"Janea's advice is valuable and full of positive energy. She shows you how to be sexy from the inside out. Feeling sexy is something you do for yourself to make you feel good and empowered; it is all about confidence and attitude. This is what *Brazilian Sexy* will show you."   —Naomi Campbell

"A simple and powerful guide to channeling your inner and outer beauty, and harnessing your power as a woman."—Kyra Sedgwick

"Everyone always raves about the French, but Brazilian women are second to none. With their beauty secrets, Janea and her sisters have transformed the way American women think and feel about themselves. They're so much more than beauticians—they change the way we look at ourselves, inside and out."   —Nina Garcia, fashion director of *Marie Claire* and judge on *Project Runway*

"Janea is not only my bikini waxer but my therapist. On her couch I discovered myself, discovered what it meant to be a truly beautiful woman, inside and out." —Hazelle Goodman, stand-up comedienne

"*Brazilian Sexy* is a great read for any woman looking to improve, and aren't we all? I have been a client and a friend of Janea's for more than ten years. I am a better mother, wife, and person because of her counsel. I eat better, work out regularly, take care of myself in all aspects. Her nuggets of advice and support keep me at my best."   —Tonya Lewis Lee, lawyer, author, and producer

Brazilian Sexy

Secrets to Living a Gorgeous and Confident Life

Janea Padilha

with MARTHA FRANKEL

A Perigee Book

A PERIGEE BOOK
Published by the Penguin Group
Penguin Group (USA) Inc.
375 Hudson Street, New York, New York 10014, USA
Penguin Group (Canada), 90 Eglinton Avenue East, Suite 700, Toronto, Ontario M4P 2Y3, Canada
(a division of Pearson Penguin Canada Inc.)
Penguin Books Ltd., 80 Strand, London WC2R 0RL, England
Penguin Group Ireland, 25 St. Stephen's Green, Dublin 2, Ireland (a division of Penguin Books Ltd.)
Penguin Group (Australia), 250 Camberwell Road, Camberwell, Victoria 3124, Australia
(a division of Pearson Australia Group Pty. Ltd.)
Penguin Books India Pvt. Ltd., 11 Community Centre, Panchsheel Park, New Delhi—110 017, India
Penguin Group (NZ), 67 Apollo Drive, Rosedale, North Shore 0632, New Zealand
(a division of Pearson New Zealand Ltd.)
Penguin Books (South Africa) (Pty.) Ltd., 24 Sturdee Avenue, Rosebank, Johannesburg 2196,
South Africa

Penguin Books Ltd., Registered Offices: 80 Strand, London WC2R 0RL, England

While the author has made every effort to provide accurate telephone numbers and Internet addresses at the time of publication, neither the publisher nor the author assumes any responsibility for errors, or for changes that occur after publication. Further, the publisher does not have any control over and does not assume any responsibility for author or third-party websites or their content.

First edition: April 2010

Library of Congress Cataloging-in-Publication Data

Padilha, Janea.
    Brazilian sexy : secrets to living a gorgeous and confident life / Janea Padilha, with Martha Frankel.
        p.   cm.
    ISBN 978-0-399-53569-7
    1. Women—Sexual behavior.   2. Man-woman relationships.   3. Women—Psychology.   4. Beauty,
Personal.   I. Frankel, Martha.   II. Title.
    HQ46.P23 2010
    646.70082—dc22   2009042837

PRINTED IN THE UNITED STATES OF AMERICA

10   9   8   7   6   5   4   3   2   1

Most Perigee books are available at special quantity discounts for bulk purchases for sales promotions, premiums, fund-raising, or educational use. Special books, or book excerpts, can also be created to fit specific needs. For details, write: Special Markets, Penguin Group (USA) Inc., 375 Hudson Street, New York, New York 10014.

This is dedicated to my clients, who I love to death; to my sisters and my mother, who taught me so much; and to my daughter, Emily, and my granddaughter, Mindla, who simply own my heart.

JANEA PADILHA

This is dedicated to all the women who think life will finally start when we lose that last ten pounds, get a better job, or find the perfect man. Thank you, Janea, for showing us that life has already started—and that it's perfect just the way it is.

MARTHA FRANKEL

Contents

contents

Foreword

By Vanessa Williams

When you walk up the steep, well-worn stairs of the J Sisters Salon on 57th Street, it's probably because the elevator is broken in the Victorian brownstone. I don't even bother to wait for the elevator anymore—it's too unpredictable.

Actually, there's lots that's unpredictable about the salon, and about the fearless Janea Padilha. (You pronounce it like "Johnny," with a French-sounding *juh*. But there's nothing French about Janea's way. She's 100 percent Brazilian.)

During the Christmas rush or at the beginning of summer, the curved staircase is jammed. Housewives and college girls jockey for space with models and actresses, rockers and debutantes, women who shop and women who never do. All kinds of people find themselves at the J Sisters Salon. Here and there a man will be peppered in, while we all wonder, *What's* he *getting done today?* People trade stories, phone numbers, scraps of information. They tell each other intimate details, and don't seem to think it's odd to do this with total strangers. More than anything, no one feels the slightest bit out of place.

Once you make it to the first landing, you're greeted by Maggie, a stylish spunky Dominican beauty who announces your arrival and points you to the waxing area. That's what first brought me to this Brazilian beauty factory and introduced me to the world according to Janea. Though Janea cannot make you Brazilian, she *can* teach you the little tricks that she has been picking up since she was a young girl, working with her sisters in salons in Brazil. And the way she looks at life is a peek into what makes Brazilian women the most sensual creatures on Earth.

Being at the salon is like going back in time. The place is antiquated, homey, and buzzing with an exotic atmosphere that's truly unique for a salon with a Midtown Manhattan address. And yet, from hair to makeup to waxing, everything Janea and her sisters do is forward-thinking and cutting-edge. I told you it was unpredictable here!

I remember when I first heard about Janea's trademark procedure, the Brazilian wax. I knew I wanted to try it out, but I worried that I would feel uncomfortable or embarrassed. But once you are inside Janea's treatment room, the whole world falls away. If you think you're there just to have hair removed, you're in for a shock—Janea gives her wisdom and keys to life in every visit to the waxing table. What could be awkward—one leg is straight up in the air and the other is hoisted on Janea's shoulder—quickly turns relaxed as Janea begins to ask you questions, and you just as easily get used to discussing your trials and tribulations in this unusual position.

From my first appointment I realized that Janea knew things. I heard her suggest that someone use a pencil eraser to get rid of hemorrhoids. How, I don't exactly know, but she said it with such authority that I'm sure it works. Tricks to relieve under-eye puffiness, a special oil to relieve dry hair, where in Brazil to get the best plastic surgery . . . those are just a few of the secrets I have heard Janea share with her clients.

Love trouble is really Janea's stock-in-trade, though. He doesn't treat you well? *Walk away, doll, and find someone who knows how great you are.* They don't know how special you are? *Stay home and make some time for you. Cook a wonderful meal, set the table, pour yourself a glass of great wine, and sit down and enjoy every bite.* Fights with your sister or your mother? Janea knows how that should work out, too. She never cares who is right or who is wrong—no, she understands that people need to get past things if they want to have a good life together. Plus, she gave me the best Thanksgiving turkey recipe, which I've been using for more than ten years. Just chop garlic and red onions, add salt and pepper, put under the skin, and then baste with butter and orange juice. Yum!

Janea is fair and kind, and being in her presence makes you

feel better about anything that has been weighing on you. She knows that being alone is better than being lonely in a relationship. She knows that life is right now, not when we do the things that we think will make us happy. She realizes that we are all special and that we have to celebrate that every single minute. She knows how to make your hair look its best, how your eye makeup can be updated, how to use less to achieve more.

On those days when you might feel bad about yourself, Janea tells you to pretend the whole world is blind! The first time she said that to me, I thought I had heard her wrong. When she repeated it, I thought she was kidding (or out of her mind!). But sure enough, when I walked outside I noticed that people weren't all that concerned with me—they have their own lives and their own problems and I could just walk along, whistling and going unnoticed until I forgot what it was that was making me feel bad in the first place. Janea knows hundreds of little tricks like that and each of them is like a small little diamond that you find unexpectedly.

Janea has such amazing style and grace. Always dressed head to toe in white, she exudes a complete self-confidence, and it's that, more than anything else, that draws people to her. Although she's a tiny little thing, she is so strong and sexy, and everyone always wants to know her secrets. Luckily for us, she doesn't feel that she has to keep them to herself. Oh no, she loves sharing them with us. And how lucky we are!

Janea's wisdom is frank, clear, and applicable. It's not wrapped in fancy paper or hard to get to. It's simple and wonderful and often life-changing. Most of all, it comes completely unsolicited. There you are in this intimate space and it's a freefall of information—even if you are just trying to focus on buffering the pain that comes with a Brazilian bikini wax. But when you walk out of her room, you will be transformed. Sometimes I walk down 57th Street, muttering to myself. "What did that mean?" I ask. Or "Why did she tell me to do that?" And then I leave it alone and let it percolate. And you know what? A few days later it will hit me, all that unsolicited advice, and it will make total sense. I often marvel at what she can change with just a few words.

What's so odd is that no matter what you go to the salon for, you wind up leaving with more than you came with!

Now, for the first time, you can get Janea's advice and logic even if you don't live in New York. *Brazilian Sexy* gives you Janea's tips, and shows you just how her advice can change your life. It's like taking a little bit of Brazil home with you, and once you've read her words of wisdom you will feel the way those of us who get to meet her in person feel all the time. You won't be tan, but you will feel as if you've spent a nice long day on a beautiful Brazilian beach, surrounded by loving friends and family.

Introduction

Growing up in Brazil, there were seven girls and seven boys in our family. Fourteen kids. Can you imagine that now? However, despite the size, my family was very close, and that came from my parents, who instilled in us a sense of respect for each other and a real flexibility in life.

For example, my father sometimes had money and sometimes he didn't. It was always up and down, up and down. At one time he was the third richest man in my town. Then one day my father came home and took my mother into another room to talk. They were in that room together for a long, long time. When they came out, my mother didn't look upset or anything. She said, "Come over here kids, I have some news."

We ran over to see what was going on. We sat down on the floor and looked up at her. "I have something great to tell you," she said.

I remember looking around at my brothers and my sisters, and everyone was staring at her, just shaking with excitement.

She said, "You know that house down in town, the small one with the red shutters?" And we all nodded, because we had seen that house hundreds of times. "Well," she continued, as if letting us in on a wonderful fairytale, "we're going to move into that house!"

There was a gasp from all us kids, and we looked to each other, our eyes wild with fear.

"Mommy, what do you mean?" we all shouted. "Why are we leaving this house? We love it here. That's not fair. That's not right. We can't all squeeze into that little house . . . No. No. No."

My mother just listened, a small smile turning up the corners of her mouth. "Of course we can fit into that house. It has three bedrooms—one for the girls, one for the boys, one for Pappa and me."

"But Mommy, where will we put all of our things? Will there be enough closets for our clothes? Will we be able to take everything with us? Mommy, Mommy, Mommy . . ." We couldn't stop peppering her with questions, all of our fears coming to the surface.

She reached out and took my father's hand. She smiled at him and then looked back at us. "You know one of the best things about this new house?" She clapped her hands together. "There's no stove in the kitchen!" I think we all screamed. This didn't sound like a good idea, believe me. But she just went on and on, her face betraying nothing. "That's right, we are going to cook outside! Yes, every meal we will cook on a woodstove in the yard. What an adventure that will be. And a lot of the time we won't have hot water, so we'll just learn to take really quick baths with colder water. And no more manicures, no more fancy dresses. Oh, this is going to be so much fun."

We were all in shock, but dutifully we packed the things we most wanted to take, and then sold the rest. We moved into that house, the girls in one room, the boys in another, Mommy and Pappa in the third. One of my sisters and one of my brothers had already married, but still—six boys in one room, six girls in the other. And those rooms were teeny-tiny. But nobody said, "I don't like to sleep with this one or that one." No, no, no, no, no. My mother said, "Let's go," and we went.

At night my father went to each bedroom before we went to sleep to see what was going on. Everybody would be in their beds, and we had some time with him to talk and tell him what was on our minds, what we had done that day. He listened so intently, as if we were so fascinating that he did not want to leave our side. It was perfect. Until the moment we slept, we got to sit and play.

When I say this, people think I'm crazy, but it was so good when my father lost his money. It was good for all of us. Knowing how much we could spend each week, knowing that we couldn't spend a penny more, that was all perfect. Also, we had more time together somehow. I guess it was because there weren't things taking us out of the house all the time, every day. We were thick as thieves. If someone said anything to any one of us about not having money, if they made fun of us or said something about my father and his money, oh boy, the rest of us would pile on that person. Believe me, no one wanted to get any of us mad.

Some of us stopped going to school so we could get jobs and pitch in to help our family. My mother would say things like, "We had meat yesterday, so today we'll have soup with beans. Yes, that will be delicious." We would watch her, and we could see that she was not sad, not angry, not fearful. And that attitude came down to us.

I remember one night my father came home and he walked in and started blowing kisses to us at the table, "Mwah, mwah, mwah, mwah, mwah." He winked at some of us, blew some more kisses. Then he got to where my mother was, cutting vegetables by the sink, and he leaned in and kissed her on the neck and whispered something to her that made her laugh. I was transfixed, biting on my knuckle, because I saw such tenderness between them, such love, such a carefree attitude. I remember that moment so well, because it told me so much about them as people, and what they meant to each other, and how much all of us kids meant to them. I remember just loving them so much in that instant.

My father eventually made money again, and we moved out

of that little house, and into a bigger house in town. And things seemed to go back to the way they had been. But not in the truest sense—because from the moment we moved into that little house, every one of us kids knew that we could do anything, that we could be happy no matter how much money we had. We knew that life could throw us big problems, but no matter what, we would be okay. It gave all of us the greatest sense of self. We still talk about that house, those times, as some of the best of our lives. My mother's laughter rang through that house every single day.

When people ask me how I became so confident and secure, I think back to that little house in Brazil. Everything about me got shaped during those years. Before we moved there, I thought I would only feel good if I had certain things—the right clothes, the right amount of room, the right this, the right that. But when we moved and I had to give up a lot of things, I started to rely more and more just on myself. And the more I leaned on myself, the more I could stand up and hold all the expectations. Learning that was life changing because when you realize that you can do *anything*, then everything becomes easier.

Now, I work in a salon, where people are always sitting around talking about their lives, maybe complaining about this or that. You know how it is—women feel like they can really let loose when they're having their hair or their nails done. They talk to their stylist in a way they often only talk to a therapist. When I first began working at a salon, I would listen with surprise, because so much of what they said had to do with not having respect for themselves, not feeling good about who they were. So years ago I started telling my clients some of the secrets I knew. Some I knew from my mother, some from my sisters or my friends, and some I knew just by being Brazilian. I would listen and then tell them something that I thought might help them.

And my clients started feeling better about themselves, started standing taller, thinking more of themselves, stopped being afraid. Then they started telling their friends that they should come to me to be waxed and also confide in me. And that's how it happened that I wound up being part waxer, part therapist! I feel as if it's my job to show women that everything they could possibly want or need is already right inside them, just like my parents showed my family. All we need to do is reach inside and find it. This book will show you how.

one

Finding Your Inner Brazilian

*How to Have Enough Confidence
to Conquer the Whole World*

From the time they were little girls, I told my daughter and my granddaughter that they are perfect just the way they are. I told them that they don't have to change for anyone—not for me, not for their friends, not for a boyfriend. No, never. I encouraged them to find their own style and stick to it, to enjoy themselves with all their own imperfections.

Some people look in the mirror and all they see are their flaws. My girls look in that same mirror and see all the good things they are, what they can offer to the world. If they hear a voice that says they are less than perfect, a voice that is making them feel bad about themselves, I tell them to put their fingers in their ears and make a loud sound that drowns out that other voice. They do not need to obsess about anything that makes them feel bad.

I tell anyone who will listen that they should concentrate on what is good. Don't like your hair today? Then make your eyes look pretty. Do not spend any time thinking badly about yourself. We are perfect just the way we are. Once you know that, you can start to really be the person you were meant to be.

Being Comfortable with Yourself

When people ask me how I have such a good sense of myself, I always tell them about my mother. I am one of fourteen kids, so my mother had fourteen different pregnancies. Fourteen, can you imagine? You can guess what kind of toll that takes on anyone's body.

Now my father was a very good-looking man, classically handsome, the kind of man that women were always looking at, always flirting with. He was charming and everyone loved to be around him. However, if my mother ever felt insecure, we never saw it. If she ever felt that her body had betrayed her, she never let on. She didn't put herself down, didn't say, "Oh, look how bad I look now, look how fat." No, nothing like that. Just the opposite. She always seemed to be in control, very relaxed about herself, never crying over small things, never making herself out to be less than anyone else.

She treated my father with a level of kindness and respect

that is very rare, and all of us kids adored him, too. She didn't look to my father to make her happy—she built her own happiness. She had a full life with us kids and was never too busy for any of us. She had great style and knew how to look good even when she was cleaning the house. She had friends who admired her, and she was highly esteemed in our town. She never asked my father, "Do you love me?" She never asked him if he thought she was beautiful or if he had looked at this woman or that one, if he thought those women were prettier than her. No, she never looked down on herself and so no one else ever did either. Her love for herself was so strong that everyone who knew her respected her, too. We could see that my father loved her and that she loved him back.

And that made me feel very secure, very much happy in myself. I saw that it wasn't so much about how you looked, but more about who you were and how you lived your life. I saw the happiness that my parents had in their marriage, and the joy they took in us kids, and that made me feel hopeful and happy.

Making Your Own Good Time

One day I had a client who told me that she felt very bad about herself. We started to talk and she told me that she had been out to dinner with her husband and three other couples, and she felt that the other women were looking down on her because her body wasn't as good as theirs or maybe her clothes weren't as nice. She wasn't sure what it was, but these women had made her feel very left out. During our session, she started to cry, and I felt so bad for her, because she is a wonderful person, and I wished I could have gone and yelled at those women for making her feel so bad.

So I told her about this party I went to in Brazil.

It was a big party, and everyone wanted to be invited. It was the talk of the town for months. Really, people would stop you in the street to ask if you had gotten an invitation yet. They would go on and on about who they thought might be invited, who might not be. When I finally did get my invitation, people were begging me to take them with me. I never had so many dates lined up in my whole life! It was so funny.

But in the end I decided that I wanted to go alone. I didn't want to worry if the person I took was having as good a time as I was, if they wanted to leave when I wanted to stay, if they would feel bad if I flirted with a man or spent time talking to some women friends. No, this was a big night, and I wanted to just enjoy myself.

There were lots of people I knew who were going to be there, and some I didn't know yet. I love that kind of party, where old friends and new friends mingle, where young and old people are dancing, where famous people and unknowns are sitting side by side, talking about the news of the day or the gorgeous woman across the room. The kind of party where you meet someone who will become your best friend and someone else that you want to kiss. And maybe you do kiss them!

So for this party I wanted to look really good, to show myself off. I was feeling good about myself, and why not show off? I don't mean that I wanted other people to feel jealous of me—no, not at all. But I wanted the people who didn't know me to think, *Who is that woman who looks so full of life?* And I wanted my friends to say, "You look the best I have ever seen you. What have you been doing? Tell me, tell me." You know, sometimes you feel on top of the world, and I wanted this to be one of those times for me.

But what to wear?

I didn't have enough money to buy a new outfit, so I went to my closet to see what was up. I had in mind what kind of image I wanted to project—fun, flirty, but not too sexual. You can be very provocative without letting parts of your body show. In fact, sometimes the less you show, the sexier it is.

I wanted women *and* men to want to be near me. I do not like when women only want to be seductive to men and they forget that half the people in the room are women. No, no, no—I am not like that at all. I would never want to be one of those women who only have men for friends, or say they don't understand women. Maybe it's because I am one of fourteen children, and there were always boys and girls around, always someone to talk to. And in my house, every one of my sisters was a really good friend to me, a really strong personality. So I have always looked up to women, and wanted to be a role model to other women. That's just the way it is in my family.

A Little from Here, a Little from There

I pulled something from this and something from that—a tight-fitting black skirt that I liked, a red blouse that was sexy, a sheer scarf, some big gold earrings. I knew the whole outfit would show me off well. I knew how I would do the hair and what color my lipstick would be, but I wasn't sure what to do about shoes. I spent a week looking at everyone else's feet, seeing what people were wearing.

Then I was walking past this store and I saw these red and white Prada shoes that would have looked amazing with the outfit. I looked at them for a long time, and for the next few weeks, had the image of these shoes in my mind. I couldn't shake it, couldn't imagine anything else that would look as good. They would have been the perfect thing for the feet, and also for the head! I dreamt about those shoes, knowing how great they would look with the outfit. But I couldn't afford them. So what to do?

I went through the closet again, and I found this old pair of white high heels. They were no Pradas, believe me. But I went to the store and bought red shoe polish. I came home and painted the shoes—not like the Pradas . . . why try to imitate something that is already great? No, I painted them in a whole new style, something that just went with the lines of the shoes.

On the night of the party I was really excited. I wanted everything to be perfect, just so. I remember that the shoes were the last thing I put on, and I thought that I had done a very,

very good job. I showed them off to my sisters and felt very proud. Everyone was smiling at me, telling me how great I looked. I twirled around as I walked out the door, showing off just a little.

I never thought, "What are you doing? Maybe everyone will be able to tell that you painted your shoes with shoe polish. Maybe you look silly . . ."

Never. Did it make me feel bad that I was wearing old shoes with the new paint job? No, it made me feel great. I felt that I was more, rather than less.

When I got to the party, everyone was kissing everyone else and I realized that maybe no one would even see my shoes, because there was such a crush of people. Later on I was standing around with some friends, just talking, when someone looked down and said, "Oh, those shoes are fabulous. Where did you get them?"

And without a moment's hesitation I told the story about the shoe polish! Everyone was shrieking with laughter, they loved this story. People were telling me that they were going to bring their old shoes to me because I had done such an amazing job. And I was so proud of myself. I did it.

At that party, I was not looking around to see who looked better than me. I was not feeling bad that I had to paint my shoes. I was not feeling sorry for myself that I wasn't in a brand new skirt and top. No, I was feeling good in every way.

Sometimes when I tell women that story, they look away. They are ashamed for me, like I didn't know what I was doing, that maybe the other women were laughing behind my back. And I tell them, "Who cares?" I am not on this earth to make other people happy about me. All I can do is be myself. And if I am true to myself, then I have done my job.

Respect Yourself

No one else can make you feel bad about yourself—you are the only one who can do that. That is the power that you have, to make yourself feel good or feel bad. Once you know that, you can stop some of those voices in your head, the ones who are telling you that you are not good enough. When those voices try to get into my head, I just push them out. I don't pay them any mind. Who cares about them?

We have a choice—we can feel good or we can feel bad. It really is up to us. If you do not feel good about what's inside of you, then you do things to fill up that hole. Some women shop, trying to fill up that hole more and more. They need Prada, they need Chanel, they need, need, need. You think those things will make you happy, you think they will make you feel better about the hurt you feel inside. But they don't. Oh sure, who doesn't like having a new dress or a great pair of shoes? But if we think those things will make a real difference in ourselves, then we are wrong. We are the only ones who can make that difference.

I have clients who tell me that they shop all the time. They buy and buy, but the one thing they cannot ever buy is self-esteem. They have to manufacture that for themselves—to imagine it for themselves. I tell them, first you do it in your head. Clean your mind out and let go of the bad, negative things that want you not to succeed.

To do this, first you have to relax. Breathe deep. Take a minute to be by yourself and dream in your mind what would make you happy. Imagine that you can look like that, walk like this, be very much yourself. Don't copy how anyone else looks, or how they want you to feel.

You also have to stop feeling sorry for yourself. *Oh, poor me, I don't have this, I want to be like that, I wish I had more of this, less of that.* Stop that. Those thoughts only confuse you. Push them out and don't let them back.

When a client tells me that she doesn't like how she looks today, I tell her, "Okay, fine. Do not look in the mirror. Not one time all day, not even to look in the glass in front of a store. No, stay away from that mirror and by noon you will forget a little of what it is that drives you so crazy about yourself. By dinner time you will be feeling a little better about yourself, and you will start to give yourself a little smile in your mind. By the time you are ready for bed, you'll forget that you can't look in the mirror, and when you go to brush your teeth, you'll look fine, just the way you wish you would. The next day the mirror will no longer be your enemy."

Sisterhood Is Powerful

I am not a competitive person. Now that doesn't mean that I don't want to do really well, be successful and all that. Because I do. Very much so. But I do it on my own. I don't compare myself to anyone. No one. When I meet a woman, I am not measuring myself against her, feeling tall only if I am standing on her back. That's not the way I am at all. The only person I feel I have to be better than is myself. I want to do better each day, each year. I want to learn from my mistakes and not beat myself up over them. But that's between me and myself. I don't have to compare myself to anyone.

I know women who cannot enjoy who they are because they are so busy comparing themselves to other women—and they feel that they don't compare well. I tell them, other women are not your enemies. Please, stop thinking this way. It's only going to make you unhappy.

I listen to women all day. And I know that in most cases, when a woman walks into a room and sees another woman, she starts clicking things off in her mind like, *Wow, she's pretty.* And instead of just enjoying that other woman's beauty, instead of meeting the other woman's eyes and smiling at her, she mentally adds, *But I'm smarter.* And immediately she feels a little better. Or maybe she thinks, *Oh, she's smarter, but I'm richer. Hmm, she's richer, but my thighs are better.* No one actually comes out and says that they think like this, but they are forever thinking that they are better than someone else if they can just find the other person's flaw. And I can tell you right now that making yourself feel better because you are making someone else out to be worse is a sure road to feeling bad about yourself. It will backfire and make you feel terrible.

I find women putting themselves and other women down very confusing, because we are all women, we all have the same problems, the same faults, and we are all trying to be treated fairly. It's hard enough to be treated fairly by men; why would we do the work of putting ourselves down? When you stop thinking of other women as the enemy, your whole life will change. Women can teach you so much, tell you things that you might never know.

I had a client come in and I could tell that she was all

the celebrity comparison

I have clients who say to me, "Do you think I look like . . . ?" And they mention a movie star or a celebrity. They want so much to be told that they look like this singer or that movie star. Or they want their hair to look like someone they see on television, someone who has a hairdresser working on them for hours at a time. Someone who has a makeup artist walking around behind them. What they don't want is to look like themselves. And I tell them, "No, you don't look like so-and-so. You look like yourself. And what could be bad with that?" There is too much talk about who we can look like—can I have her nose? Can I do my hair like hers? Can I change my body to look more like that one? People need to stop trying to be anyone but themselves. And to be happy with that.

wound up. "What's the matter?" I asked. She told me that her best friend had just gotten a huge promotion at work. "Oh," I said, "you must be so happy and proud for her."

She didn't say anything for a long time.

Finally she told me that no, she wasn't happy for her friend. She wanted to be, but she found herself very jealous and upset that her friend was now doing better than she was.

"But you can't measure yourself against anyone else." I said. I could see she didn't believe me. I told her the following story. A woman is at a dinner party and she sees another woman at the opposite end of the room. The other woman is very pretty, with beautiful hair and gorgeous skin. There are a bunch of people sitting around her, hanging on her every word. The first woman starts to get angry, and thinks, *What does that woman have that I don't? Why is that woman so popular and I'm not?* Instead of going over to see why everyone is so attracted to that woman, she stands all alone and has a terrible time. When people try to talk to her, she doesn't answer them. When a man asks her to dance, she ignores him. Finally, some people move, and she sees that the other woman is in a wheelchair!

There are always people doing better than us, and other people that are doing worse. That is just the nature of life. And those things change—one day you're up, the next you're down. You have a good job and your friend doesn't—a year later you're out of work and your friend is the boss of her own company. This happens all the time, like a seesaw. But if we begrudge people their happiness, than we will not get our own.

It's not like happiness is a pie, and if someone eats a big piece then you don't get any. No, happiness keeps expanding. We have to root for our friends and for other women to succeed, even if it means that they do better than us. In the same way, we cannot become obsessed with our enemies failing. In fact, we should forget about the people we don't like and not worry about how they are doing. And remember, it doesn't make you better when people do worse.

Lighten Up on Yourself

It seems to me that women are always killing themselves over something. Is there one woman who doesn't say, "My life will start to be good *as soon as* . . . "? And then they have a dozen things that fit in there. *As soon as* I lose ten pounds. *As soon as* I make some more money. *As soon as* I find the right man. *As soon as* I finish remodeling the kitchen. *As soon as* I start working out every day. They give themselves no leeway, no avenue to feel that everything is good just the way it is, right now. If their kid doesn't do well in first grade, they are already talking about how he won't be able to go to a good college. If they sleep in, they feel like the whole day is ruined. They are so rigid that sometimes it seems like they might just snap.

I had a client who came in one day in baggy pants and a huge shirt. I could see that she was feeling very bad about something. We started to talk and she finally told me that she couldn't stand herself because she had gained a lot of weight after she stopped smoking. She told me that she didn't want to buy any clothes in this big size because then she would be committing to being fat, that maybe she wasn't going to lose the weight and she would always be that heavy. She could barely meet my eyes, and she was crying so hard.

I told her that she had to stand up straight, not hide her face, and embrace this great thing she had done. To stop smoking is a huge accomplishment. There are people who try for years and years, and she had done it. So be proud, not ashamed. The extra weight? It will go away.

I made her promise that she would go out and buy some pants that really fit her, some blouses that were not so big that two other people could be in there with her. Because oversized clothes do not make you look smaller, despite what a lot of women think. I wasn't saying that she should wear skintight clothes, but she should wear something that really fit, that flattered her. Buying clothes in her right size will only make her feel better, not worse.

When she walked into the salon a month later, she looked like she had lost half the weight. When I asked her how she did it, she admitted that she hadn't lost one pound. But because her clothes looked so much better on her, it made it seem like she had slimmed down. She was standing straighter, didn't have the big circles under her eyes. She looked like all the weight of the world had been lifted. She was finally able to see herself for the dynamic, wonderful woman she was. She stopped apologizing for being overweight, and she realized that when people saw her, they liked what they saw. No one was judging her the way she was judging herself.

See with Your Heart, Not Your Eyes

My mother told us every day how wonderful we were, how smart and pretty. She taught us to be kind to people who had less than us, and to respect all people for what they are, not what they had. And that feeling stayed with me always.

She taught me not to concentrate on my problems, but to see the good in the situation. Yes, I have the same problems everyone else does, but I don't give them the time of day. I close my eyes to them, because otherwise I might be miserable. I only look at the good things—that I am a good sister, mother, grandmother, friend. That I do the right thing most of the time, and that people like being around me. What more could I ask? That's what I think of as Brazilian confidence.

two

Hair Today, Gone Tomorrow

How Less Is Really So Much More

More than anything I am known as the woman who invented the Brazilian wax. I'm very proud of that, because I think that the Brazilian wax gives women more confidence and makes them sexier, cleaner, and more self-assured. So if I have to be known as something, I'm happy to know this is what it is!

Girl from Ipanema

Okay, I'm going to tell you how I came to invent what is now called the "Brazilian wax." Years ago I was on the beach in Brazil with my husband and some friends. We were sitting around on the sand, eating and talking and laughing and drinking, just having a fun day. I can remember everything about that day because it became such an important day in my life. It's almost like that thing where you say, this happened *before* and that happened *after*. So this is the before part: We were having a wonderful afternoon, everything just perfect, and then I saw this woman walking toward us. She was absolutely stunning—great hair, beautiful body, every part of her looked perfect.

I continued talking to my friends, but I kept my eyes on her because she was so striking, the kind of woman who exudes confidence, who makes both men and women want to be in her orbit. I like women like that, because they make other women feel good about themselves. At least I think so.

She had a beautiful smile and she was smiling at the people who were sitting at the table right next to ours. She came over to them, kissed them all, and then she sat down on a bench with them. She opened her cover-up so naturally and it just slipped off. There was something about her, the way she seemed so comfortable in her own body, that kept me transfixed. It's always wonderful to see a woman who seems to own herself, who isn't adjusting her clothes or looking like she wishes she could fall through the earth. No, this woman just looked like she was so happy with herself. Then she leaned forward and put her elbows on the table. She was talking to her friends and gesturing and laughing. And she just relaxed her body, the way you do when you're not self-conscious, when you think no one is looking at you.

She was wearing a very tiny thong bikini. I remember how natural she looked, how sure of herself, and how beautiful her body was. I can still see the fabric of that thong, the blue cotton the same color as the water, with tiny red dots. It's seared into my mind, because right then, as she leaned forward, her butt cheeks relaxed, and I saw it—this line of hair that went all the way up the sides of the thong! A lot of hair. More hair than I could have thought could be on that part of the body. It was such a surprise to me, because I had no idea that women had hair like that.

It was one of those moments when everything gets quiet. I was twenty-six years old and I had been in the beauty business since I was twelve. My sisters and I had been around women in all kinds of dress and undress, and yet I had never seen anything like that line of hair. Never. No one had ever mentioned it to me, either. I thought maybe it was just that woman, but then I started asking myself if it was possible that I had the same hair as her. And if I looked the same as her when I was wearing a bathing suit. Did other women have it? I wanted to check it out, but I was pretty sure that I didn't, that I wouldn't find anything. Because wouldn't I know? I mean, really, how could I have hair like that and not know it?

When we got home, I went into the bathroom, locked the door, took off all my clothes and squatted down above a mirror. And sure enough, I had that same line of hair. Just the same as that beautiful woman on the beach.

Of course women don't know about this hair, because it is

truly the one place on our bodies that we never see. And I started thinking how much better it would look, and how much better it would *feel*, if that hair was gone.

I thought about shaving it, but then I remembered how itchy it feels when the hair grows back after you shave. I thought about cutting it, too, but the same problem—it would be so itchy. I was up almost all night, thinking, thinking. My sisters and I all worked in my aunt's salon then. So the next day I went to work and closed the door to one of the treatment rooms and put a mirror down on the floor. I started applying hot wax on that area and pulling it off with strips of muslin, a tiny little bit at a time. Tiny, tiny. I'm telling you, it took me over three hours to finish the job! It was hard to figure out which way to pull the cloth because everything was backward in the mirror. And it was hard for me to hold the skin very tightly the way I do it in the waxing room now, so that there's no pain. This was the craziest thing, but I was determined to do something that would change this hairy situation.

My sisters were dying to know what I was doing. They kept asking me through the door, "What are you up to?" I just kept saying through my gritted teeth, "I'll be out in a few minutes." They couldn't imagine what I could be doing, alone, for all that time—but I didn't tell them. Not yet. I had to see how it all looked when it was done.

Although I had been around waxing for years by that time, I had never done one. We had a girl at the shop who did all the waxings. She did the bikini wax, where you get rid of the hairs that might sneak out in a bathing suit, making the triangle of pubic hair look neater. But this was different, this was getting rid of all the hair you *never* see. So what a way to do my first one, right? It was trial by fire! But as soon as I was done, I could not believe how great it felt. It was amazing. The sensation was so exquisite, so soft and frictionless. And it looked so nice and neat. I could see my whole vagina, and right away I knew that it would be a very easy way to take care of myself. It would be so much more sanitary. It was as if I was aware of my vagina in a way I had never experienced. It made me feel so powerful. Oh yes, I was very pleased with what I had done.

I came right out of that room and went to talk to the girl who did the waxings. When I told her what I had done, she screamed. She thought I had lost my mind. She had never put wax between the cheeks like that, and she couldn't believe I had put it so high up, too. She was so surprised and didn't know whether to laugh or cry. I wanted to show her what it looked like, but she was not interested.

For the next few months I tried and tried to talk her into letting me do it to her, or even having her do it to me. But she kept resisting me. I kept asking my sisters, too, but they said they would wait and see how it grew out, how it looked when it was a couple of weeks old. I did it to myself again when the hair grew back, and this time the waxer let me show it to her. And that was it—right then she realized how great it looked and she agreed to let me give her a Brazilian wax. She was so nervous, but I did it really fast, really well, and when it was over, she went wild. She absolutely loved the way it felt. Of course it was so much easier doing it to someone else, and I was thrilled that she could do if for me in the future, that I never had to squat over that mirror with my tiny strips of muslin.

I felt such a triumph, although I wasn't sure what was going to happen, if we would ever find other women who would want to join us.

But I didn't need to worry—the waxer started to convince her clients to give it a try. And every single one of them loved the results. It just feels so good. And then I started to urge the clients who came to me for haircuts or facials to do the Brazilian, too. Some of them were reluctant, but one by one they started doing it. No one ever complained; in fact, everyone we did it to started to spread the word. It made them all feel so clean and also sexy. And then we realized that no one wanted a bikini wax anymore, they all wanted the Brazilian! It was like this not-so-secret club, and everyone in it was so thrilled and wanted to say that they did it before anyone else.

So Brazilian waxing started to become popular in Brazil!

[TIP]

Never, ever try waxing at home. This is one procedure that must be done by a professional. Even though I developed the Brazilian on myself, at least I had a history in beauty work. Trust me—hot wax on delicate skin should only be done by someone who knows exactly what they're doing and who can see exactly where they're putting it.

Moving to New York

When my sisters and I moved to New York City and we opened the J Sisters Salon, I went into a bit of a tailspin. In Brazil, I had been doing more than fifty haircuts a day. I also did makeup, facials, cutting eyebrows with scissors so they look much neater, all those kinds of things. But I didn't speak English very well. How can you give someone a haircut without talking to them? In Brazil, I always explained what I was going to do, and in New York, I couldn't, so I thought and thought about what would be the best job for me in the salon, a place where I could fit in. I wanted to pull my weight, but I was afraid that I wasn't going to be able to. And then finally I decided, why don't I become the person that does all the waxings?

That's how I came to be the main waxer. I did the bikini wax on my clients, because that's what the women knew and that's what they wanted. But with every client I would take some time and try to convince them to do the Brazilian. I would explain how clean it makes you, how easy it was to keep yourself like that, how much better sex would be. But they just kept saying, "No thanks, I don't think so."

There I was again, doing the Brazilian on myself!

But I am the kind of person who doesn't give up. So I kept pleading, and it took me one year to convince one client to do a Brazilian. When she said yes, I started to scream with happiness. Listen, I understand that it is hard enough to open your legs to a man in the dark: Imagine what it's like to open your legs to a

woman in the glaring light? The way we do the Brazilian is that
you hoist one leg up on my shoulder, and bend the other one,
so I have total access to every part of your private area. I understood that women would be uncomfortable—after all, we are
taught to keep those parts hidden and never seen. Women are
very vulnerable in this position, so I have to be very aware of
respecting them, because the first time they always look like they
would rather close their eyes and sink into the floor. The women
who do this the first time, I always tell them how brave they are,
because it's true. It's a hard thing to put yourself into that position in my room.

The day my client finally agreed, I wanted to make sure she
was at ease. The waxing only takes a few minutes, but when I
put her leg on my shoulder, she couldn't look at me. But I kept
talking to her and eventually she was laughing with me and
telling me a story, and I knew that she was fine with it.

I was so happy. It seemed to me like I had passed some kind
of test, that something really important had happened. I had this
silly grin on my face.

I didn't charge her, because she was my first. It was a Friday,
at around ten in the morning. I ran in to tell my sisters and
they were happy for me, because now I wouldn't be bothering
them to do it all the time! A few hours later my client came
back into the salon with five friends. She had been out to lunch
with them and, while they were sitting in the restaurant, told
them what I had done to her, and every one of them wanted
to try it. I did the Brazilian on those five women—they were

happy and I was thrilled. What a day. It turned out that one of those girls worked at *Elle* magazine. She loved the Brazilian and had someone write a three-page story about it for the magazine. It was a very big deal for us, for the J Sisters Salon, and then the floodgates opened and everyone started calling, asking for an appointment with me.

Here's the thing—I'll admit that when I did that first Brazilian on myself, I did it because I thought it would look better. I just didn't want to look like that woman on the beach. What I didn't know was that there are lots of other results—some amazing things happen. First of all, it's a lot more sanitary, because you can just wash that area and get it really clean. No more hair to interfere. When you wipe yourself, nothing gets tangled in your hair. It's as if you were never really clean before. Additionally, when you have a Brazilian, you don't have a lot of discharge out of your vagina, and it's a lot cleaner.

Do It for Yourself

We have clients who do not come to the salon for months at a time. We think maybe they have died. When they come back we say, "What happened to you? You disappeared." And they'll say, "Oh, I didn't have a boyfriend, and I thought I didn't need to have a waxing. I just met a new guy, and before I sleep with him I want to get a Brazilian." They know how important it is. Because it feels better, both for the woman and the man.

But also I have clients who realize that they don't need a man to have a waxing. They can do it for themselves, for their own vaginal health, to feel good. It makes them feel so confident. It's a funny thing—no one knows you've done it, and yet

how good it feels

I'll say this: Most women are not taught to take care of their vaginas. Maybe it's because mothers don't talk about it to their daughters, so the girls don't know what they're supposed to be doing. What's the right thing, the wrong thing, soap or not? How would you know? And then these women have daughters, and they don't talk to them about their vaginas, either.

I was lucky because my mother used to watch us after the shower. She would ask us if we had cleaned our vaginas, and if we said no, she would tell us to go back to the shower and do it. No one was embarrassed by that, it was just like any other part of the body. It's very important to keep your vagina clean. I'm talking about the folds of skin outside. My mother told us that we didn't have to use a lot of soap, but that we had to be sure that we rinsed really, really well with lots of water. And that we had to do that every single time we took a shower. She told us that the vagina lubricates itself, and that water was okay to just keep it clean. Sometimes I say that to clients of mine who are in their forties, and that is the first time they heard this. And they are thrilled to have more information.

And when they come back, they tell me that I was right, that they are cleaning themselves in a way they never did before, that sex is better, that they feel better in many, many ways.

you feel so much more sure of yourself. They want to be able to see what is going on, to be in touch with their vaginas. I have a client who brought her sixty-year-old grandmother in to get a Brazilian. The woman had never had any kind of waxing, and she was very nervous. I talked with her and calmed her down, and then I did the waxing. She loved it so much. "How could I live sixty years without knowing about this?" she kept asking. She comes in all the time now, without her granddaughter, just to get one. She's told a lot of her friends and some of them are clients now.

The Best Part

The Brazilian is great for all the reasons I told you, but here's the best part—the Brazilian makes sex so much better, because there is nothing between you and your man. Whether he is just stroking you or you are having intercourse, the sensation is heightened. Everything is so much more sensitive. Your lover can concentrate on the spot that feels good without having to move the hair away. It really is amazing. Beyond amazing, actually. Everything about it feels terrific. Women tell me that it makes them so much more orgasmic and that they enjoy sex in ways they never knew possible. That's why once you have one, you'll keep it up. You won't want to go back to the way it used to be!

Still at It After All These Years

I never get tired of doing the Brazilian. My clients still love it,
and every time I talk someone new into it, I still get a thrill,
because I know they will like it so much. It isn't some kind of
fad, something that will change as skirts get shorter or longer.
No, it will always be great. And it's not about what others think.
I know from experience that women sometimes think they are
doing it for a man, but then they realize that they like doing it
for themselves. They love the feeling, the smoothness. My first
Brazilian wax client is sixty now, and she still comes in for a
waxing all the time.

three

Muss-Free Brazilian Glamour

*How to Make Yourself Good in
Minutes, Not Hours*

Brazilian women are very focused on how to be sexy. It's not how to be sexy by wearing certain clothing; it's how to be sexy in your attitude. We don't care if you are a size two or a size twenty. Yes, we want to look good, to take care of ourselves, but we know that it isn't only about having the "perfect" body. You see women in Rio and they each have a different body type. Some are round, some are straight as a stick, some have thick waists, and others have their bones sticking out. Some have breasts that spill out of their tops, others are flat as boards. Some have hair that is thick and luxurious, and others not so. The only thing that is the same about them is that they each walk around like they are the best, the sexiest, the most incredible. That's the thing about Brazilian sexy—it doesn't take hours and hours of fussing. No, it's the opposite.

A Little of This, a Little of That

Everybody has their own little home remedies for looking good, their own little tricks. Some women will tell you to scrub your face and others will say, no, no, don't ever do that, that is absolutely the worst thing you can do for your face. One woman might say that you should use olive oil on your hair and others might say no, it will spoil and smell and you'll never be able to get it out. Some women will tell you to use this cream or that, and they might give you a little jar of it, something they made in their kitchen. You might use it for a week, then another person will say, no, mine is better, and they will give you theirs.

My clients come in to the salon and say, "Please, please tell me what your beauty regimen is." I tell them, but they think I'm not telling the whole story, that I'm holding back a little bit. But the truth is that when people ask me what my beauty regimen is, I laugh at that expression, "beauty regimen"—doesn't it sound like you're in the army and if you don't do it right you'll get thrown out? Or worse? I imagine all these women lined up in a row, applying mascara to their eyes, or moisturizer to their cheeks, or dark lip liner. And if they get it wrong? They have to do twenty push-ups! No, what I do is not a "regimen." It's just some of the simplest things in the world.

No one ever knows what works best for them. And that's an important thing—whatever works for one person might not work for another.

I'm going to teach you some very easy, basic things that make my skin and hair look great—with the minimal amount of work. My clients love these secrets—see if they work for you, and be willing to try a variety of techniques until you figure out your own best "regimen"!

First, Clean Skin

I'm compulsive about my skin being clean, because I believe that you cannot have a clean soul with dirty skin. First the skin, then the rest! Happiness. Flexibility. Forgiveness. Be good. That's my idea of a healthy, clean soul. And I believe it starts with clean skin.

Even though I work in a salon, I have no time to lay down in a bed for somebody to give me a facial. I just don't have time. And if you get a facial and you don't take good care of your skin, then two weeks later you will need another one. The trick is to take care of your skin every day.

So I do this by myself: Every morning I wake up an hour before I have to leave my house. I spend about half an hour thinking about what is going on in my life. Then I wet my face and I get toner, the cheapest one I can find. I put it on a cotton ball and I clean my skin with it. Just toner and cotton. I rub it all over my face, behind my ears, on my neck. I make sure that every part of my face is clean, because that's the most important thing—then you don't get blackheads, pimples, and all the other things that happen when your skin isn't spotless. I just make sure that the skin is as clean as possible and then the breakouts happen less often.

Then Soft Skin

When I was a kid, I watched the women on the beach in Brazil. As they sat there talking to their friends, or tickling their children, or kissing their boyfriends, they would take sand and rub it onto their arms and legs. It was almost an unconscious thing. But I was watching. I was fascinated. And I started doing it to myself.

It hurt a little bit, but when you were done every part you had "sanded" felt incredible. I would do my arms and legs, and then my shoulders and my stomach. When I found out how good it could make the bottoms of your feet feel, I used to bring some sand home from the beach and rub it in every day.

Those days at the beach, it was like sanding my whole body, getting rid of all the dead skin, all the imperfections. I would get my sisters to rub sand into my back. I'd walk into the water and wash all the sand away. And I would feel so fabulous. And then when I would get home from the beach, I would just take a quick shower, put on a little moisturizer, and my skin would feel amazing. It was so soft that I couldn't stop touching my arms. When your skin is clean and soft, everyone wants to touch it. You can see it yourself, that even you want to run your hand up your own arm or down your leg. It's so sexy when your skin isn't flaky or dry. Everyone looks at you and smiles when your skin looks soft and smooth. And the older you get, the skin gets drier. So you want to take care of your skin every day.

Now I live in New York, and I'm not able to go to the beach a lot. So I have this thing I do—I scrub my whole body with a hairbrush! People always say, "What?! A hairbrush? That must be so painful!" But it's not. It's similar to using a loofah.

I use a natural boar bristle brush. It gets rid of all the dead skin and it's fantastic for your circulation. I get into the shower, wet down my body, and then use it everywhere except my face. I scrub my body probably three days a week. I love those days. It's very much like using the sand on the beach. Then I rinse off and wash very quickly. Too much hot water and too much soap will dry your skin out. Less is more. I know people who take these long showers, or long hot baths, and then they complain that their skin is dry. I tell them to make it snappy. Hurry, hurry, hurry. Cooler water, and not a lot of it. That's the key.

There are also some really good dermabrasion products and you can use them, too. If you use them once a week or so on your hands, you won't believe the difference. All the cuticles get sanded off, all the scaly skin gets washed down the drain. Your hands look years younger, and feel terrific. But the hairbrush works just as well. And it's cheap and easy. I don't like to make things more complicated than they have to be.

Treating the Face the Way It Deserves

There are all kinds of things I've learned over the years, little things that stayed with me. Like how we have to treat the face very gently. It's not as tough as, say, the skin on your shoulder or legs. Not at all.

The skin around the eyes is especially fragile, much thinner than any other skin on the body. The worst thing you can do is pull at it, stretch it out. So I just use a good cream on the eyes, and I very gently pat it on. No pulling the skin, just tap tap tap with your finger.

On my face I use a good cream, too, one that isn't very thick and lets my skin breathe. I use a cream for wrinkles. But I use the very minimum. I have a busy life, so what am I going to do? Take hours to make sure that there's not one wrinkle? No thank you, I'll do what I can but I know there are many more important things in life, like spending time with the people I love.

If I get an itch on my face, I use the heel of my hand to scratch it. Never do I use my fingernails. Oh no, the face is not the place for that, it's too rough on the skin. It's one of the things I notice in American women, is that they touch their faces all the time. If you go to Brazil or to Europe, you will see that women never touch their faces. Never. They know this makes your face oily, or causes blackheads, or smudges makeup. No, it's just not good. So I'm aware of never pulling at the skin or touching it when I don't have to.

I never, ever pick at my skin. If I get a breakout, I leave it alone, just rub it with the toner. Women tell me that they think they need to squeeze the blackheads or the pimples, but believe me, they will go away on their own. When you pick at it, you just make it last longer, not shorter. Don't look at it if it makes you crazy!

Also, and you're going to laugh, I try not to move the muscles of my face! I try not to make funny faces. Otherwise the skin is going to be a mess. Touching the face is a problem, and making faces, too. I think it stretches out the muscles, and they don't go back to the way they should be. Why take a chance, right? I'm not saying I don't smile and laugh, but I don't pull my face into funny shapes.

I also spend a half hour a day or so every day out in the sun. Even in the winter, I make sure to get outside, walk, feel the sun on my face. In the summer, same thing. I make sure my arms are uncovered so they get some color, too. Nothing too much, but a little color on my skin feels good. Now even doctors are saying that you need the sun to get all your vitamin D. I'm so glad, because I hated it when they said we shouldn't be in the sun at all. I think we need to be outside and not hiding in the shadows. We need to turn ourselves toward the sun.

You have to figure out what makes your particular skin look best, not what made that other woman's skin shine. You can give a technique or product a month or six weeks, but if you don't like the results, try something else.

How Hair Can Make Us Feel So Good

I had this client once who came in and said, "You have to dye my hair blond." I stood back and looked at her. "No," I told her, "your skin tone is all wrong for blond." "I don't care," she said. "I want you to do it." But I said no, insisting that it wouldn't look good. She kept saying I had to do it. Back and forth. "Why blond?" I kept asking.

Finally she told me that she thought her husband might be having an affair. Oh, then I understood—the mistress was a blonde and my client was competing with her! I finally gave her a great haircut and calmed her down. I told her that she was a strong, wonderful woman. A brunette woman! And if her husband preferred blondes, then maybe she was the wrong woman for him. That was years ago and they're still together. She and I are still laughing about that.

If I know anything, it's that women are more obsessed with their hair than anything else. You see them fluffing it, playing with it, putting it behind the ear, then in front, then in back again, all day long.

Without a doubt, when your hair looks good, you feel better. Women love having someone blow out their hair or high-light it or cut it. I hear it every day—my clients just feel so much more appealing when their hair is styled. And why not? It's often the first thing that people notice, and when your hair is dirty or sloppy, when it looks limp and straggly, you give the wrong impression. Some people can do it themselves and it looks great; others need to go to a professional to get that same look. But either way, it's important to make sure your hair is styled, even if you just blow it out and clip it back.

Quick and Easy

Some women spend a lot of time fussing with their hair—others just grab a clip, pull it back, and make it look effortless. I don't have a lot of time to fool around with my own hair on workdays, so I wash it a couple of times a week, and most mornings I either just brush it out and pull it up into a ponytail, or I leave it down and put a hairband on it so the hair isn't in my face, in my eyes. I know that some people obsessively wash their hair every day, but mine doesn't look good when I do that. It gets too limp. This is another thing that you have to experiment with—what works best for you, every day or twice a week or less? I have clients that look best only washing it once a week. Once you know what works best for you, your hair will look so much better.

When you have short hair, you may have to blow-dry it or

style it two or three times a week so it looks good. You need it to have a good shape and have haircuts often. You have to make sure that the ends are always healthy. For me, I like to keep my hair long so I can get away with doing less. For work I can pull it back and it looks really neat, and at night I can do an updo a hundred different ways. It gives me a lot more flexibility.

I don't use a lot of products on my hair, but that's because I have really thick hair and I don't need to. If my hair was thin or straight, I would find the best product for my hair and use it so that it gave my hair the best lift. I get a haircut every six weeks so there are not a lot of dead ends and it looks healthy and good with very little work. Haircuts are so important. You have to keep that up.

If you color your hair, make sure that you keep that up, too. There's nothing worse than hair that has roots that are four inches long. You should make sure that if you color your hair, it looks right with your skin tone.

Making Up

I think makeup is a very personal thing. As women, a lot of us like playing with it, trying this color on the eye or that one on the lips. It can be a lot of fun. But it's not the number one thing to make anyone beautiful. More important is to be secure inside. That beats all makeup. I remember one night I was invited to a party, but I worked late. I didn't have time to do my makeup or my hair, didn't have time to decorate my body. But what am I going to do, not go to this party? Of course not. I knew my soul was beautiful, so I went. I pulled my hair up and put a flower in it. I put on a little lip gloss, and that was it. Boom, I was out the door. And you know what? I had a great time.

You have to believe in yourself. Makeup is supposed to enhance your beauty, not disguise it. It's supposed to make you

easy eyeliner

I do think that a line of eyeliner looks terrific, either above or below the eye or both. It makes the eye pop and look very attractive. I used to stand in front of the mirror and as I put the liner up to my eye, the eye would start to close up. So sometimes the line was thick, other times thin. Never the same from one side of my face to the other, and never the same on top or on bottom. Then one day I was playing on the bed with my granddaughter, and she had this little mirror. I leaned over it, and it was amazing—my eyes weren't squinting. I realized that when you looked down at the mirror instead of straight ahead at it, your eye stayed open. I went to my bag and grabbed an eyeliner and looked down at that mirror and drew a line under my eye. Perfect. Then I did the top line, and the same thing—perfect. I took the liner off and then did it again and again. And each time I was so happy to see that it worked perfectly. This was one of the best things I ever discovered. When I tell my clients this trick, they immediately go get an eyeliner and they lay a little mirror down on a chair or a bed and stare down at it. Then they draw the line. And they agree—this trick is foolproof.

look like yourself, only better. It's supposed to cover up all the little imperfections that we have. For me less is better, but some people are happier when they have a full face on. I understand that. Some women can make themselves look so fabulous with makeup. They make their eyes sparkle or they make their cheekbones look so prominent and striking. I love to see women like that. But other times, makeup can make you ugly. You know what I mean, the women who put it on wrong and they look silly. They put on so much that you can't see their faces anymore, all you can see is the makeup. No, that's not good. I think of makeup as the thing you might do on the days you need a little lift. When I go to a party I like to put on a colorful lipstick, but I don't believe that lipstick makes me. Without the lipstick, I am still myself.

Mind, Body, Spirit

The body is important, sure, but to have a good life means taking care of the heart, the head, and the body so we can be sexy in all things. It's to take care of what's inside of us as much as what's on the outside. So I'm careful to make sure that I am living well, taking good care of all the other parts of me, not just the face and the hair, not just the body. Yes, I keep the body in as good a shape as I can. But what's the point in doing that if my mind isn't clear? And what's the point of keeping the mind good if I am putting bad food into me every day? It all has to be balanced.

Brazilians work very hard to eat well. I have people say to me, "But you Brazilians eat so much meat." And I laugh, because it's true that if I throw a party, you can be sure there will be a steak or a roast. And sometimes I take those steaks and fry them, one at a time, washing the pan out in-between each one so I can get it very hot and the meat really sears. It's delicious. But when I put it on the table, it's just one of the many dishes.

I eat vegetables a lot, both cooked and raw. Sometimes I simply steam some vegetables in a little chicken broth, some garlic, and a little black pepper. I use whatever vegetables are around—zucchinis, squash, broccoli, whatever. I make sure to only cook them for a minute and a half, so the vegetables are still very crisp. I put that on a plate and sprinkle some white vinegar over it. That's a big favorite in my family. Oh, it's so simple and tasty.

There are always big bowls of fruit in my house, whatever fruits are in season. I cut some up to have at every meal, and I also grab something to take with me in the car, an apple or an orange or a banana. And there are nuts and nutcrackers on the table always. It is such a fun thing, to sit around with family and friends and pass the nuts around. Walnuts, pecans—they are all really good for you, really healthy.

Brazilian people also eat a lot of guarra nut powder. It's a little fruit that grows in the Amazon; it has a black seed that you put in the oven to dry and you make it a powder. You can put it in your coffee or into juice. It's very healthy and gives you energy, makes your stomach feel right.

I personally eat a lot of acacia berries for energy. It's recently become very popular in America because people think it makes you thin. I'm not sure about that—but I do think it makes you horny!

And I eat a lot of cilantro. Cilantro is very important for stamina, and if you eat it every day it gives you the get up and go you need. Some people like it, some don't. But I put it into salads and it's terrific. Very refreshing. I eat lots of hot peppers, all different kinds. They have been demonstrated to be good for the stomach, and also for your mood—they make you happy!

I love food because it gives people so much pleasure. And what could be sexier than that?

four

Walk Like a Brazilian

How to Make Your Problems Go Away

One of the things I learned when I was growing up was not to wear my problems on my shoulders like a heavy shirt, and not to let that shirt bring me down. Listen, I have problems just like everyone else. The president, the people who clean the streets, no matter who— we all have problems. We are human beings and things don't always go the way we wish they would. That's just life. But I don't like to live as if those problems own me. We cannot focus solely on the problem, making it such a big deal that it overwhelms us. No, if I have problems, I learned to toss them off my shoulders so that I could walk tall. And the taller I walked, the less the problems seemed to matter. I think of this as the Brazilian way—not only to look at the happy things, but to make the bad ones fade into the back, so you hardly notice them anymore.

Don't Worry, Be Happy

Sometimes I have family problems, sometimes work problems, sometimes love problems. Just like everyone else. But even if I am really overwhelmed and sad, you can't tell. I hide it from everyone, and even sometimes from myself! No matter what is going on in my life, no matter how I feel, no matter if I have a broken heart, or I wish I could stay in the house all day in my pajamas, you would never know. I do not carry on if I make a mistake, or if I can't find love, or anything else like that. No, never. I never wear my heart on my sleeve. No, I smile and act like things are good. And then something funny happens— things start to get better.

I don't want to be unhappy. That's a choice I have. And I choose not to be miserable. I think that worrying makes us ugly. Yes, I do.

Instead of worrying, I like to spend half an hour every day thinking through my problems, trying to figure out how I can change this or that, trying to see what I might do to make things different. I sit by myself for thirty minutes, whether it's in my house in the morning or in the salon between customers, and I run through the ideas in my head. I picture myself without the problem, see what that feels like, how I can go about getting that. I breathe slower and relax my body so I can understand what might work to get this problem settled. Some people tell me they do something similar to this, and they call it meditation. But I just consider this my way of figuring things out.

Every day after I think about my problems and what I can do to fix them, I forget about them. I don't let myself obsess about the little things that bother me and push me down. I don't like to give my problems so much value. I sweep them under the rug, and I go about my day. I don't even think about that rug all day. When I come home, I notice that rug doesn't even have a lump underneath it. Gone!

Problems Are Opportunities

Sometimes a problem can be small but we can make it into something much bigger. I recently had an appointment to meet someone and I had to cancel many clients to see her. She was coming to my house. At the last minute she called to tell me that she couldn't make it. What am I going to do, kill myself? Or say bad words about her and tell all my friends how she had made this plan but then she didn't come? Oh, poor me, poor me, poor me . . . Yes, I know some people will do that and wallow in that.

But that's not the way I am. Instead of making it into a problem, I thought, okay, I have an unexpected day off. I think I will make dinner for my sisters and some friends from out of town. I never could have done this if that woman had come over. I went shopping, bought all this food and wine, and spent the day cooking. My sister brought some Brazilian friends who I hadn't seen in a long time, and we had a fantastic evening. There were seventeen of us around my table. I told everyone what a great thing it was that this woman had canceled on me. I wanted to thank her for not coming. I wanted to kiss her for giving me the chance to have this wonderful night. So that thing that I had thought was going to be bad turned into something just the opposite. And I see that happen all the time. We just have to open our hearts to the possibilities and not close them shut and play the victim.

Think of Problems as Your Friends

Problems are also what make us stronger and better. You don't look back and say, "You know, things were absolutely perfect last year, and I learned a lot from that. I really grew." No, you learn from the times in your life when things are hard and yet you got through them. You showed your strength, you didn't fall apart, and maybe you found out some good things about yourself or your partner or your friends and your family. You found a strength that you never could have imagined you possessed. And you should be proud of that. You now know what you are capable of, and it is more than you thought last year. Things scare you a little less now because of that. And the problems don't seem like a mountain you can't get around.

Look Your Problem Right in the Eye

Some people think that what I mean is that we should pretend we don't have problems, but that's not my style. I like to handle my problems head-on.

Let's say I am having a problem with someone, a friend or a family member. Maybe they are mad at me because I said something that insulted them. Or maybe I am upset because I heard they had a party and I wasn't invited. You know how those things can start to fester, like a splinter in your hand that begins small and a few days later is so bad that you cannot bend your finger.

The first thing I ask myself is, what do I really want to happen? Do I want to stay angry? Because sometimes digging in and being right sounds much easier than solving the problem. I can tell everyone that I was so hurt by Karen, and that Karen isn't a good friend. I can repeat the story over and over again to anyone who will listen, and each time I tell it Karen will sound a little worse. After a while, I will forget the real thing that happened between me and Karen, because the story will become bigger than the little fight we had. And all my other friends will rally around me and stroke my head and tell me that I'm a much better person than Karen and that I don't need her in my life.

Or maybe I'm embarrassed that I did the wrong thing to Karen, and I don't want to admit it. Sometimes a very little thing gets blown up, and what started as a little comment becomes a much bigger deal.

So the choice I always have is that I can do nothing, or I can call Karen and do one of two things: I can very simply say, "I am so sorry that I did anything that made you feel bad." Or I can honestly tell her that she hurt my feelings. And hopefully we will come to a better place. So I can make it right, or I can *be* right. My choice.

I tell my clients all the time that they are much more in charge of their lives than they believe. They can make things work out the way they want if they know what it is they would like to see happen.

I am always trying to make sure that what I want is the best outcome for me and for the other person also. I picture the person and me together; I imagine the story all the way to the end, where I can see us sitting down for a meal, happy and enjoying ourselves. I can feel sorry for myself or I can move forward, and I am always in favor of moving forward—straightening things out and making that particular problem go away. Or if I can't make it go away, at least it's now in the backseat, not in the front.

You Can't Fix a Problem That Doesn't Belong to You

I have a client who told me, "I didn't come here for six months because my boyfriend told me he needed a little break. And that was horrible, because I wasn't sure what was happening. And then he came back, but all we did was fight. A few weeks later he broke up with me. He said that I was not a good girl-friend, that I was selfish, ugly . . ." She told me how depressed she had been for those six months, and that she didn't feel worthy of getting pampered and waxed. She told me more and more of the bad things that the boyfriend said and did to her.

I listened to her for a while. She just kept talking about the things the boyfriend said, the terrible way she had felt since he left, how her self-esteem had walked out the door with him.

"So, is it true?" I asked. "Were you a terrible girlfriend? Are you selfish? Because I already know you're beautiful, so he was wrong about that."

I saw a little grin pulling at the sides of her mouth. "No, I was a great girlfriend. I thought we were very happy together. But now I think he was cheating on me, and instead of admitting it, he turned it on me. But when he said that I was . . ."

I stopped her. "Why do you fool yourself when he says he needs a break? Who ever needs a break when they are happy? You knew right then that he was going to leave you, right? Right then you knew your relationship was not good. But you didn't listen to yourself, right?" She nodded, her eyes down. I picked her face up so she was looking at me.

I told her the following story. Once I had this boyfriend who would leave and then come back, leave and then come back, leave and then come back. My head was spinning by how

many times he was in and out of that door. I told myself I didn't
know what was going on. But I did. I told myself that if only
he would stay, everything would be fine. But it wasn't. One day
I had enough and I threw him out. He said terrible things before he left. For some reason I just let those words settle over
me like a scratchy wool blanket. And even though it felt awful,
I held it tight against me, as if that was what I deserved.

For the next few months I felt horrible. I didn't go out, I
didn't call my friends. No, I just shut myself up with his anger
and let it echo off the walls, telling me over and over what a
failure I was.

But eventually I woke up and I thought, *If I don't get out of
this house and have some fun I am going to just go crazy*. I called a
few of my girlfriends but they were busy that night. What
should I do? I had heard about this restaurant that was supposed
to be really fabulous and I wanted to go there. But no date.
Should I? Shouldn't I? Oh, what the hell. I called and made a
reservation for two people at nine o'clock. I didn't have a date,
but why should I announce that to the whole world? No, I told
them that two of us were coming.

I went home after work and I got out this really pretty dress
that I love. I hadn't worn anything nice in a long time, and it was
so good to remember what I looked like. I pulled up my hair
and put on a little eyeliner and out the door I went.

I was nervous but no one could tell. No, I held my head high
and I walked into that restaurant as if I owned it. The maître d'

sat me right away at a nice table. I ordered a glass of wine, and while I was sipping it, I kept looking at my watch. Where could my date be? What was holding him up? The waiter asked if I wanted to order, but I said I would wait a little bit longer. A man at the bar smiled at me and I smiled back. Then he sent over another glass of wine. I held it up in a silent toast. Then I looked at my watch again. After a while the chef sent out a small plate of appetizers. I nibbled at them. Finally the man from the bar came over. "Did your date stand you up?" he asked. "No date anymore," I said. He asked if he could sit down, and I said yes. We wound up talking until they closed that place. It was one of the best nights I ever had. This "date with myself" was fantastic, and it brought me right back into the world.

My client started to laugh when she heard this. I asked her, "Why did you let that boyfriend call the shots on you? Why are you feeling so bad over what he said? Why wait for him to make you feel good? You have to do that for yourself. This is his problem, but for some reason you have chosen to take it on as yours. Why would you do that? Is it because you don't have any problems of your own to be thinking about?"

We talked for a long time. I told her that I worry that if one person can make you feel so bad about yourself, then the next one can, too. If you let someone's problems be yours, well, there's no end in sight. Because how can you fix a problem that has nothing to do with you? You can't.

The next time I saw her she looked fantastic.

Perfect Doesn't Live Here Anymore

I listen to a lot of my clients who are frantic that things are not "perfect." Their marriage is not perfect, their children are not perfect, their job is not perfect. They keep trying to get to that place where perfect lives. And they never do. My attitude is that things are never, ever perfect. And that they never will be. Maybe we wouldn't want them to be, either. Maybe life would be boring if there was nothing left to do or to change.

I think of life more like an airplane, and you have to constantly be adjusting the steering. A little this way and a little that. If you think that it's bad when things are not exactly how you expect them to be, then you will always be disappointed. You will always be thinking that you did something wrong, that you are a failure, when it really has nothing to do with you.

Two people can hear the same story, and one person thinks it's okay and the other thinks it's a terrible problem. Which of those people do you think is sleeping better at night? Which of them do you think is living a happier life? Which of them is healthier? If you think of everything as a problem, then it becomes a problem. Everything will fall on your head and you will be overwhelmed. But if you think of everything as just part of a bigger picture, it tends to not be as scary. You can look at each thing and not be afraid so much because you will figure out what to do.

I was taught to not worry about the little things. My family had good times and bad, and what others might call big problems, sometimes. If I was upset about something and I told my mother what was bothering me, she would say, "Is that all you have to worry about? There's nothing else going on for you to think about?" She made it seem not so important. So I learned to let all the little things go away. It was a good way to look at things. Believe me, it's got to be a huge problem for me to get worried. The rest of the time, I just shrug it off and go about my day.

Maybe you thought things were just terrible and right then something wonderful happened. Bad to good. You have to be able to change your mind about things, to flip around, to be flexible. That's why you have to make sure that you are in charge of the problems, and not the other way around

Stand Tall: Only You Know What's on Your Mind

I always take care to stand strong. When I walk in the street and I see women slouching along, heads down, shoulders hunched, I want to walk up behind them and pull their shoulders back, pick their chins up, tell them that if they are going to look like a sad person, then sadness will stay right at their side, it will move right into their house.

I'll tell you another thing—people are not so interested in you as you think they are. No, really. Sometimes you think that people are looking at you or they're talking about you or they're checking out your clothes. But usually they're just completely in their own heads. They hardly notice you. That's a good thing to remember.

When I was growing up in Brazil, people would be in the street and everyone would say hello, how are you today? People really looked at each other, smiled, commented on what you were wearing. So when I came to America, I acted like that. I was always saying hi, complimenting people if they looked good, engaging strangers in conversation. But people would turn away. And it made me feel bad, so I stopped. I started to

hold your head high

I try to always present myself to my best advantage. I have enough attitude to fill this world. But even I am overwhelmed by things sometimes. So I have this other trick I do. When I am feeling bad—maybe have a lot on my mind and can't seem to shake it, or if I can't figure out what to do about something, or if there's a big pimple in the middle of my forehead—I just pretend that everyone in the world is blind! This is such a great way to walk around. Yes, people are standing right next to you, but they can't see you! So you can laugh at yourself, you can act funny and crazy, and no one has any idea. Yes, the whole world is blind to your troubles, and then this happens—you become blind to your own troubles, too. You start to feel lighthearted.

My clients love this trick and they tell me that it changed their lives because they had been so self-conscious, and then they stop worrying about what people are thinking of them.

walk like everyone else in the street, head down, no eye contact. And I realized I was miserable. It wasn't the way I am. So I went back to my Brazilian ways, and you know what? I stopped caring if people thought I was acting strange. I stopped worrying. And eventually I noticed that people were treating me really well. I have met some wonderful people that way.

If you walk around like you're confident, then things will sort themselves out. People respect you more and treat you better when they think you're doing well and that you are happy. What do you Americans say, put on a happy face? Yes, it works. People want to be around successful, upbeat people. Don't you?

Pretending costs nothing, and it can do so much for your sense of self.

five

Cry Yourself an Amazon River

The Cheapest Therapy in the World

When we were little kids and we were upset over something and we would start to cry, my mother would hold us, rub our backs, and say, "Go ahead, cry it out." She would keep handing us tissues and stroking our heads. She never told us to stop, to put the sadness away. No. She understood that if you push that unhappiness down, it will come out somewhere else. When I hear women telling their kids, "Oh, stop crying, stop acting like a baby, stop showing your emotions," I get very upset. Because I know that is very bad advice. Our emotions are not something we should be ashamed of. No, I feel that we have to claim our sadness and turn it around. Crying does that. It lets you control something that feels very uncontrollable. And that control adds up to something that moves you forward.

It's All Right to Be a Crybaby

I had a client whose husband died suddenly. She was in her early fifties when it happened. It was a terrible, terrible shock, because he had been healthy and very vital. And they had one of those relationships that people are always jealous of and wish they could find—they liked to play tennis together, they traveled all over the world together, they walked down the street holding hands. He was romantic with her and used to surprise her with presents or handwritten notes, that kind of thing. Some women live separate lives than their husbands, but she was not one of those women. So when he died she was really at a loss.

For the year or so after the funeral, she kept talking about how she couldn't get her life back on track anymore, how she wasn't interested in anything, including their children and grandchildren. I felt so bad for her because she was in a horrible, deep hole. She was sad because she lost her husband, but even more because she had nothing to do, nothing to look forward to. And that kind of depression can be very bad, very debilitating. "My life is done. I can't be happy again," she kept saying.

Every time I saw her, I never said, "Please don't cry." Because what would be the point? She could not see her way out of this place, and no amount of talking would change that. I watched her get sadder as time went on, and I was worried for her. I kept thinking of what I could do to help her.

One day, after months and months and months of her terrible unhappiness, I said, "Okay, you know what might be good for you to do? When you leave here, go home. Pour yourself a drink. And not just a little one—pour yourself a full tumbler. Put on a song that you and your husband loved, something that will make you feel really miserable. Maybe it will be your wedding song, or the song you both sang out loud when you were driving in the car, or the song he always played to make you laugh. Put it on once and then repeat as many times as you want. Sip the drink and listen to the song. Sit down on your couch and make the time to cry for one hour. Just the crying—no answering the phone, no getting up to see what's in the refrigerator, nothing else. No, you cry, and you wail, and you let yourself wallow in it. This is your turn to cry because your husband has died, because you cannot go anywhere with your life. It is like you are dead, too, like you died with him. Only you have to keep living, which is sometimes worse. Cry for this. Cry for not being able to grow old with him. Cry until your eyes are swollen shut. But after an hour, you get up. You wash your face, and for the rest of the night, you do not cry at all. Not one bit."

She was giving me this look like she didn't know if she could do this.

"Tomorrow, you do the same thing," I told her. "The drink, the song, the crying. But now, take out the old photo albums. Look at all the good times you had together. Look at how happy you were. Scream, beat your hands on the arm of the sofa. You can use the whole hour if you want. It's up to you. But one hour only."

I told her to do this same thing every single day for a month. And I knew that day after day, the crying would become less. This is our nature. Putting the time aside is such a good way to really submerge yourself into the grief, and to start to feel better.

I didn't see her that month, and I was concerned for her. But then she came in to the salon and she looked completely different. "How are you?" I asked.

She said, "You know, I thought this whole idea was crazy. I had been crying for so long, and those first few days I felt really foolish. I kept looking at the clock, like it held the answer. I wanted to just stop with the song and the drink, but I didn't. I got over my embarrassment, and I really let myself get into it. Each day I noticed that I was crying for less time. Each day I felt that I had to dig deeper to feel the pain. Then I realized that as soon as the crying was over, I would wash up, leave the house, and feel good for the first time all year. I went to see my kids and played with my grandchildren, and realized I hadn't done that since my husband died. Yesterday an amazing thing happened. I poured the drink, I turned on the song, I sat down, and . . . nothing. I waited, but I didn't feel like crying any more. I didn't feel like beating myself up over how my life was over. I listened to the song, I didn't take a sip of the drink, and I put some of the photo albums away. I love my husband still, but I don't feel like I went to the grave with him. I can see now that I will go on living and that maybe something nice will even happen in my life."

You see, it is a very fast therapy, and look at all the money you save! And in the end, you are better.

Crying Instead of Begging

This cry therapy works for all kinds of things: a breakup, a divorce. I have clients who get divorced and they say, "What am I going to do?" I tell them, "Enjoy it! You are not the first or the last person to get divorced." They tell me that every single thing in their house reminds them of the ex. His this, his that. They tell me that they don't want to even go home because the house smells of him.

I tell them to clean him out, get him out of there. He may not be in the house anymore, but he has certainly taken up residence in your mind. So you have to change things around. If the furniture reminds you of him, move it into a place where he never was. You take the couch from this wall to that one and all of a sudden he's not sitting on that couch. If you can still smell him in the house, light candles. Lots and lots of them. If you both picked out those towels, give them away. If you cannot live with the things that remind you of him, then be strong and think of yourself first. If less of his things are staring you in the face, suddenly you don't think of him all the time. He starts to get out of your hair.

You do this and you do the cry therapy. Think of the things he did to you, how bad he made you feel, how embarrassed you were when you found out he didn't love you the way you thought he did. Think about those nights when you sat up waiting for him and when he came home, he looked a little fuzzy on the edges, like maybe he was kissing someone else. When you asked, he told you that you were crazy. And you started to think that maybe you were, even though he smelled of a perfume you never wore.

Cry.

Think of the good times, too, because that helps with the crying. Remember how it was in the beginning when you first met? Remember the sex? Remember how much you laughed together? Don't push those feelings down—they belong to you and no one else knows how you feel. The good part about the cry therapy is that you don't have to talk to anyone else about it. It's yours, all yours.

We carry so much inside of us, and we need to let it out. If we let it sit there, it makes us more unhappy.

Believe Me, Life Goes On

Sometimes when you go through a breakup, you cannot see that you will ever feel good again. Sometimes my clients just mope and mope, but they don't really give in and feel bad for themselves. They just act like they will never be happy again. So I tell them this story that I heard in Brazil: There was a woman whose husband died. She loved him very much and she could not stop crying, could not seem to find her feet again. Nobody and nothing could make her feel better. She stopped eating and just sat in her house all the time, thinking about him. Then she had an idea, so she went to a local woodworker and asked him to make a sculpture of her husband in wood. It took him months, and she went by every day to see if it was coming out well. She described her husband in detail so he would know exactly what he looked like.

When the sculpture was done, she was elated because it looked exactly like her husband. She set it up in the living room and put candles and statues of the saints around it. It became an altar to her husband. Every night she would go there and speak to him and cry, and she made him out to be a saint, too. She told herself over and over that she would never be happy again

This went on for a long time. She cried herself to sleep every night. But eventually she came back into the world a little bit at a time. She started stopping in to some of the shops in town and chatting with the owners. Then she went to church and saw some old friends. She let her sister make her a meal one night. Little by little, step by step.

Then one day she was in town getting groceries, and she met a man. They stopped to talk for a little while on the street. A few days later, she ran into him again, and he took her for lunch at a small café in town. He made her laugh, and it had been so long since she heard that sound that she almost didn't recognize what it was! And then a few days later he knocked on her door and asked if he could come in. He brought her flowers and she was happy to see him. She asked him if he wanted a cup of coffee and he said yes. She went out to the yard to get wood to light the cookstove, but the wood was all gone. She looked around outside but there was nothing to burn, no little pieces, no big ones. She went back into the house and looked around. And then she saw the sculpture. Without even hesitating, she put the statue of her dead husband into the fire and burnt him so she could give her boyfriend a cup of coffee.

I heard that story when I was young, but I understood what it meant even then. You have to let go of things that no longer serve you. Life has to keep going; and everything has to change. That is the one true thing in this world. So you cry, you carry on, and then you pick yourself up and move on. When you are sad, when something horrible happens, you have to say to yourself, "Okay, I'm going to cry for one month or one year, and I am going to cry hard. I am going to cry like no one has ever cried before. I will be puffy and swollen, I will scream and yell, I will be the most miserable I can be. I won't be on anyone else's schedule, and I won't listen to them when they tell me this isn't good for me. Because I know that there's an end in sight! After a year, I will throw away those tissues and go forward." And one of the added benefits of the cry therapy is that while you are crying, you start to remember who it is you are, what it was that made you happy in the first place, and how much better you can be in the future. It's like through those tears we get to glimpse our better selves, the better us.

Flush Out the Sadness

The best thing we can do for ourselves when we are sad is to act sad. But our whole society says that's not the right thing to do. People say things like, "Get over it" or "Get on with your life," as if sadness has an expiration date. Or they try to pretend that something that hurt them so badly can just be pushed aside. This cannot happen. You must feel what you feel and feel it wholly. Otherwise it will come out somewhere else. I have friends who get stomachaches or headaches, and they are always looking for a reason. They go to this doctor and that one, always looking for the doctor to tell them the cause. But the doctor can't find anything. When they finally admit that they are feeling sad and they give in to that, the stomachache or headache miraculously goes away. This isn't surprising to me at all.

But when you are sad, your friends and family get very uncomfortable, because they feel that we should have control of our emotions. How silly. We are better off knowing that our sadness is ours, that we own it, that we can give into it and it will not destroy us. I have seen so many people get better, both physically and emotionally, by just admitting that they are sad and crying their eyes out.

The truth is that crying is healthy. Sometimes, even when things are going well, I feel the need to cry. I always feel that we need to cry to be moist. And to be moist, we need to cry. When that happens to me, I call my sisters and my daughter and I tell them that I need a day to myself. I don't want them to come over and give me a hug, I don't want them to talk me into going out and doing something fun. No, I need this day to cry. I get into my pajamas, and I prepare myself, getting ready to feel this sadness and crying. It's almost like I am full, and I need to get it out. I start to think of all the things that make me sad. I need to prepare myself to pull gallons of water from inside of me. I think of everything that is on my mind, everything that can make me sad, whether it's about love or money or business or anything else. I prepare myself mentally and then I get very comfortable physically. I give myself the whole day to cry my eyes out. This day is mine and that's what I'm going to do.

I always think I'm going to cry for the whole day. But what happens is I cry for fifteen minutes and I feel so much better, like I threw up. I'm a new person. Okay, let's change the energy. I call my sisters, I call my daughter, and I say, "What are you doing? I want to come meet you!" I feel so much better. Crying therapy—done.

You have to make the time to cry. And like most things in life, when you make the time for it, you have to go all the way. This is the one time that it's okay to feel sorry for yourself. You do that, you cry, you wipe your eyes. That's the only way it works.

six

Go with the Flow

How to Be Flexible

There's an expression in Brazil: "You cannot dance rock 'n' roll to a samba song." Meaning that if you dance to the right song, your life will be easier. Instead of fighting something, you go with the beat, not fight the current so much. You will be happier. My clients have problems. I have problems, too. Who doesn't? I tell them, enjoy your problem; eat this problem for breakfast and for lunch. Gnaw on it like it's the most delicious thing you ever tasted. You'll figure it out. When you get out of this problem, you're going to take a look back and you will be so proud of yourself. This is how we grow and learn to be happy, not by having things go along without us falling into the water.

Live with What You Have

Money is too important to some women. I hear it every day, women who are having trouble breathing or taking care of their kids because their husbands aren't making as much money as they used to.

I have a client who came from a family with a lot of money. She and her husband had two kids, and her husband had a good job, he provided very well for her and the children. She didn't work, and she loved being a stay-at-home mom. Things were going good for them.

Then her husband's business started to not do so well. He had never taken any money from her family, but when these hard times came along, she went to her family and got some money for her husband. This was her idea, not the husband's. And he told her it would take a year or so before they knew if the money made a difference in the business.

A few months later she was in the salon and she told me that things weren't going so well. "How come?" I asked her. And she told me that she respected him less because now he was using her money.

Truthfully, there are very few times that I don't know what to say, but this really made me shut up. How could it be that she was mad at him for something she had caused to happen? How could she think less of him? The man had taken care of her for all those years, and now he needed her help. Instead of standing strong behind him, she was acting like a spoiled little brat. I finally found my voice, and I told her the story of my mother and father, and about how money never ever came between them. Just the opposite—they became closer the harder things got. And I told her that the best thing was that when things turned around for my parents, when they got more money and went back to a bigger house, my mother never said anything bad about my father or blamed him for what had happened. She always treated him with so much respect, and he treated her the same. She was part of this unit, our family, and this was what was going on within the family.

I told my client to enjoy the moment. Maybe she had more time with her husband now, maybe she could find out more about his business that would make her closer to him, to stop being angry with him and instead show him more support. Well, she started to cry—I could see she was embarrassed. And when I saw her a few months later, she said that their whole life had turned around. She realized that she had been acting scared, and that her husband deserved much more of her than that.

Learn to Accept Change

I had a client who was very unhappy with her husband. She had been miserable for fifteen years, and finally she decided to get a divorce. She was a wonderful, soft-spoken woman. Her husband was very critical of her, and she had started to believe him when he told her how worthless she was. So I was excited for her that she might find a little happiness when they decided not to be together anymore.

The divorce took a long, long time to complete, and he wouldn't leave the house until it was all done. So she felt like a prisoner. But I told her, "Call me, we can go out for dinner some nights, or just go to the movies by yourself. Don't let him call all the orders."

Every time I saw her, she was counting down the time. And then one day it happened—the divorce was final and her husband moved out. I was so thrilled for her. And I thought she would be dancing in the street.

But instead, she went into a big funk! She spent all her time worrying about money, about being alone, about not having someone to come home to.

I told her that yes, she lived alone now. She would walk into the house and no one would be there. She would have to learn to live with less money. All that was true.

But what she gained was that she could look in the mirror and not feel bad about herself.

No one would be telling her that she wasn't good enough, smart enough, thin enough, curvy enough. Take a class, learn to do the samba, do something for yourself. Grab change with both hands and enjoy it. That's the Brazilian way.

It took her some time, but she finally embraced her freedom. She learned that life never goes the way we think. And that doesn't have to be a bad thing. In fact, it's usually good. We just need some time to catch up with the changes.

Treat Your Children Like Kids

I hear a lot of my clients worrying about their children. Will they get into a good school? Will they do well once they get there? Do they need tutors? Do they need to play sports, even if they don't like to play that game?

And what I see is that women treat their infants like adults and their teenagers like babies. I'll give you an example—I went out to eat with my granddaughter one night. Next to us was a couple with a little baby, maybe seven or eight months old. The baby was sitting in a high chair, drinking out of a bottle. The parents were talking and not even looking at the baby. The baby was holding his bottle so awkwardly. Please. I wanted to go over there and hold him, but I couldn't. The parents would say, "He can do this by himself. He has to." But to me he was just a little baby who needed to be fed.

I had a client who was doing her daughter's homework because she was afraid the girl would fail! I told her that a little failure wasn't the worst thing that could ever happen to her. Had my client never failed at anything? What is so bad about failure? Sometimes the best things come out of what we might consider failure, like when my father lost his money. My client admitted that she had, but felt that she had to protect her child. I pointed out that doing the homework would actually be hurting her daughter, because when the daughter got into college, she wouldn't even know how to do the basic work.

Now my client's happiness is not so tied up in her child's

perfection. And because of that, the daughter is doing better in school.

When We Can't See Our Own Noses

I have this client, who is very, very successful. She's beautiful. Smart. Funny. Everything is good about her, even the luck in her life. But she didn't see it that way. She wasn't particularly sad, but she wasn't happy, either. She always had this look—head down, eyes down, like she was saying to herself, "I'm nothing." I used to say to her, "Get out of your own way. You are beautiful, you are a lucky girl, many people would kill to be in your place. You have everything you wanted. So you have to know the power you have inside of you; but you need to put your head up and live your life at this moment."

She tells me, "My manager is mad at me. He wants me to do this thing that I don't want to do. And my agent is mad at me because he wants me to do this project, too. But I'm not so sure about it. I just don't think it would be good for me. But what am I going to do? I can't have them mad at me."

I put my hand up. "Wait, who's in charge here?"

She tells me that she has to listen to them, that they are smarter and know more than her and blah blah blah. I say, "Really? Because you seem like a smart girl to me. And you know your business. Why do you let them make all the decisions? If you think this is the wrong thing, then don't do it. And don't let them push you around—you are the one who makes all the money for them. Clean all the fear that you have out of you. You are professional, you are successful, you must be happy in what you do. Forget about everything else."

Well, she was a good listener. She talked to me a few times the next few days, and talked herself into it. She marched into her manager's office and told him, no, she was not going to do that project. And although he gave her a hard time, he backed down. I see her these days and she is completely different.

Don't See Your Own Flaws

One day this same client told me, "I'm very pissed because I'm going to work with my ex-boyfriend. And I don't know how to do that." And I said to her, "This time, forget about him being your ex-boyfriend. He's going to be your partner at your work. Do your best." "But I have to kiss him," she said. "Kiss, hug, do your best," I said. And when she came back from shooting that movie, she had such a big smile. I feel proud for her. She's happy now, because as long as she pulled every good thing that she had inside, she became herself. Now she knows who she is.

I believe that's the way that people have to think about life. Everybody has bad and good things; all of us. But I just think about my good things; I forget about the bad ones. Because what good would it do if I walked around thinking of every flaw I have? What would be the point? I would just make myself miserable. And everyone around me would be that way, too. No, no, no.

In this life, we have to get it right. And that means being proud of who we are—walking tall, being the best we can. And when we fail? Be flexible! Keep moving, put on a smile, and forget that anyone might be watching!

seven

The Brazilian Woman's Guide to Men

*Learn How to Sculpt Your
Diamond in the Rough*

Every woman I know wishes she could change some things about her man! This can range from the way he dresses to the way he wears his hair to the way he treats waitresses or how much he tips. Some women spend all their time fighting with their man about these things. But that seems like such a waste of time. I tell my clients to take the easier route, and to gently steer their man into the direction they want them to go in. This way everyone wins, and no one feels like they have lost anything. I think of men as diamonds in the rough, and it's up to us to shape them!

I Wish My Man Would . . .

I love listening to my clients talk about their husbands and boyfriends. They tell me all the good things about them—how funny he was at her friend's house the night before, what a good time they had on vacation in the Grand Canyon last winter, the beautiful bracelet he surprised her with for their anniversary.

And then they start to tell me the things that drive them crazy about those same men!

The first thing I always ask is, "Are you happy with your man?" Because if the woman is already out the door in her mind, well, then there is not much to do. She should probably just keep walking, and they will both be better off. If you are changing someone just because you can, this will not work. You have to really care about the person, and you have to want the change to work out better for that person.

But if she tells me that she wants things to get better, that she is truly committed and loves her man, then so much can change and all those things that drive her crazy will go away. I tell my clients that, really, there are so many things that they can teach their men. And even if the man isn't aware that he's learning—like how to dress better, how to be more courteous, how to groom himself—he'll be happier with the end result.

Clothes Don't Make the Man—But They Don't Hurt

With clothes, I feel sorry for men, I really do. I mean, we women have each other to talk to—Does this look good on me? Does this skirt show off my butt well? Do you think these pants are too tight? We know that we can ask other women and they will help us chose the thing that shows us off in our best light. We know that clothes can enhance us, make us look more powerful, more beautiful, more interesting.

But men don't know that much about clothes. And they don't talk to other men about it or organize expeditions where they head to the mall with other men to see what's new and what would look good on them. No, they don't have that sounding board.

Women start dressing themselves and picking out their own clothes when they are young girls. They like to try on pretty dresses, hats, jewelry, all of that kind of thing. They decide very early in their lives if they feel comfortable in dresses or if they will wear pants most of the time. You see little girls fighting with their mothers in the store—they are already sure of what they want and don't want to be told to wear something else. Their minds are made up by the time they are five or six.

But with men, their mothers probably bought them all their clothes when they were young. And maybe all the time until they left home. They have no idea what looks good on them.

Maybe he was never even taught about what would look good on his body type. Maybe he doesn't even know that he has a body type! Maybe he still thinks he looks good in the clothes that he bought fifteen years ago. Or in college. And maybe he has never looked in the mirror and been critical of what he's wearing. Maybe he doesn't really see what clothes can do for him—he just thinks of them as a uniform. He wears them, but he has no affinity.

Very often a man wears the same thing every day. If he goes to an office, he wears a suit and a tie and a shirt. But he doesn't think, *The cut of that one suit works better than the other. I should stop wearing those old-fashioned shirts and get something more modern.* No, it's just his uniform. He takes a shirt from the drawer, a tie from the rack, a suit off the hanger. If he works with his hands, maybe it's the jeans and the work shirt, day in and day out. If you didn't know better, you'd think he only had one of each, because they look exactly the same. Exactly. But that is not his fault, the same way it's not my fault that I don't know how to fix a flat tire or how the engine in my car works. If I needed to know those things, I would hope that someone would help me without making me feel stupid.

I bet neither his mother nor any woman in his life has ever taken the time to show him that clothes can make him look so much better, and that he can start looking forward to wearing them. But in order to make clothing not his enemy, you have to go about it in the right way. For example, if you say, "You know, that shirt probably looked good on you when you were

a teenager," then right away he will be on the defensive, getting angry and self-conscious. Then he will do the exact opposite of what you want him to do. Trust me, that blue shirt you
can't stand? He will never take it off! He will wear it all day,
every day. You will wish you never mentioned it. So you have
to be smart.

Your man doesn't want to be nagged or embarrassed or
ridiculed. No, no, no, that will only make things worse. Much
worse. Really, who wants to be nagged?

Instead, start with some conversation that goes around the
real thing you are thinking. Maybe you can show him a magazine ad, and mention that you think that pair of pants would
look good on him. Just a quick little thing, no big deal. And the
next time you are out shopping, you buy him a pair of pants like
those. "I bought those pants you like," you might say. He might
be surprised, a little confused, but because you don't make a big
deal out of it, he probably won't either. When he wears them,
you say how nice they look—but very offhand, as if you're always complimenting him on his clothes. Then maybe you buy
him a shirt that is the kind you wish he would wear. When he
puts it on, you just nod and smile. "Looks really good," you tell
him, very casually. Later that day, you might compliment him
again, but don't go crazy, don't show him how important this is
to you. Because that will scare him, and then his antenna will go
up and he will start to get suspicious.

I know this sounds simple, but it is the way you do it that
makes all the difference. That first shirt looked so good, you just

had to buy him another. And what a surprise, it was on sale, so you bought another in a different color!

Eventually, the clothes you like start to outweigh the ones you hate. You can start to weed out the bad things from his closet. You can say, "You know, you never wear this anymore, let's give it to charity." One day you'll realize that he's dressing the way you like, and he won't feel like you manipulated him. And the best part of this is that he will find that he understands clothing better, that he likes the way he looks more than he ever did. Because clothes don't make the man, but they can sure make the man look better!

Really, That Ponytail Has Got to Go

I had one client who said to me, "I swear my husband looks like a caveman. How can I get him to get a good haircut and to cut the hairs that grow out of his nose? It makes me sick."

This is another area where you have to be careful. No one wants to be criticized about how they look. Even the most secure people will feel bad. If you tell him, "You have to do something about your hair," he will feel uncomfortable. And it won't make him want to go out and get a good style. So I told my client to go about it like this: If you think his haircut needs to be different, go with him to the salon. Tell him you want to spend the afternoon with him and make an appointment. Nothing out of the ordinary. Mention to the stylist that you think it would show off his gorgeous face better if his hair was cut shorter on the sides, or whatever it is you think he needs. Don't tell her that his hairstyle has been the same for twelve years, don't make it you and the stylist against him. No, that will backfire for sure. When it's done, compliment him. All month you can casually mention how handsome he looks. But don't let on that you couldn't stand the way he looked before.

The next time he goes back for a haircut, mention how great his hair has looked. Tell him to tell the stylist how much you liked it. Trust me, he will come home with an amazing look. Because whether he says it or not, and whether he even knows it or not, he wants to please you, in the same way that you want to please him. And now this one problem is solved, because he's not going to want to go back to the hairstyle that didn't have you telling him how good he looks.

Some Places Hair Should Not Be Growing

As for grooming, this is a little more delicate. If you want your man to trim the hair in his nose and in his ears, you have to think of some way to do it without offense. If you say, "You know, Judy's husband Harold trims the hairs in his nose, and I think that looks great," oh boy, you are just asking for trouble. Because no matter how sure your man may be about himself, he'd be thinking that you like Harold, that you think Harold is more handsome than he is, that maybe you want to sleep with

Harold. I mean it, men are very soft inside. They look hard, but we know better.

So what you have to do is compliment some guy that doesn't present a threat. Maybe you see some man on a television show that both you and your man like. This way it's not a guy that he knows; it's not a guy that he would run into on the street; there's no competition. And he's not a guy you would ever think of sleeping with.

You can point out this guy on television and say, "Hmm, doesn't he look handsome? Wait, it looks like he cuts those hairs in his nose. And you know what? I think he gets his eyebrows trimmed. That looks good, don't you think?"

Probably your man won't jump up and say, "Oh yes, honey, that would look great on me! Let me call my buddy John and tell him about it. We can go to the salon first thing in the morning and have it done together." Wouldn't that be funny? But no, men aren't like that.

But it does put the idea into his head. Maybe the next time he looks in the mirror he notices that he has hairs growing in strange places, and he wonders if he should cut them or have the stylist do it for him. When he goes for his next haircut, I bet he asks the stylist to trim some of those hairs. When you notice it, don't start screaming with joy. But do mention how good he looks, how much more modern. If the stylist is smart, he or she will keep trimming the hairs in your man's nose and ears without even asking. But because you have very easily talked about it, it is no longer such a big deal. He won't be embarrassed and he won't feel that he's the only one in the world that has those things. And that makes all the difference. I'm telling you, this is the way to get what you want without all the fighting. And everybody wins.

That client whose husband needed to be groomed better came in a couple of months later and said it was like a miracle. She said her guy looked so much younger, so much more contemporary. She said those little touches had made such an enormous difference. And she said she was thrilled to be seen with him. All that over a few little hairs.

It Doesn't Hurt to Hold That Door Open

I had a client who was upset that her husband had stopped being a gentleman to her. She told me that when she first met him, he would hold the door open or carry her packages when they went shopping. She said that if she went to the bathroom at a restaurant, he would stand up when she came back and hold her chair out for her. She liked those things, and said they made her feel very special. Somehow, a little bit at a time, he had stopped doing those things.

"I liked it when he did all those things. It made me feel special. I'm not a fragile flower, but I still like to be treated like a woman."

I asked her if she thought that maybe she had stopped treating him like a man, and so he had stopped treating her like a woman. She thought about this for a long time and then she nodded. "You know what? I don't do the little things I used to do for him anymore, either. I know he likes this perfume, but I can't remember the last time I put any on. He likes me to get dressed up sometimes, but I can't remember the last time he saw me in anything but T-shirts and sweatpants."

She decided she wouldn't say a thing to him, just start remembering what she was like when they first fell in love. And the next time I saw her, she told me that he had gone back to treating her the way he had when they first met. She said their life was a lot more fun again. She changed, and then he changed, too.

You see? It's two ways on this street, and we have to give to get.

eight

What Men Really Think

How to Make a Good Relationship

I have a lot of friends who are men, men who know that I don't want to go out with them or have sex with them. Only once that is out of the way can men be friends with women. These are men that I feel really comfortable with and I can talk to them about lots of things. I go out to dinner with them, or they stop into the salon and sit and talk with me for hours. Some are old friends and some are new, but either way, I ask many many questions of them. I ask them all about women. I mean, really, how can I tell women how to be happy with men if I don't know what men are thinking? And I'll ask anything, because absolutely nothing embarrasses me.

I want to know what they like, what they don't like, what

they look for in a woman. I want to know what we, as women, can do to make good relationships. What we can do to make them happy. And what we can do to make great sex with them.

For Men, the Question Is: Do I Want to Sleep with Her?

From talking to them, I now know what is the biggest difference between men and women. Let's say a woman walks into a party. First thing she does is look to see what all the other women are wearing. We care about what other women think, and we want to see if there is something new and exciting, a new haircut, a new style of dress. This could take only a few seconds, but she will be aware of who is there, how they look, who is talking to whom. Women dress for other women. They wear a nail polish color that they think other women would like, that kind of thing. That's just the way we are, like birds preening for one another.

After she notices the women, then she looks around at all the men. She sees a guy with a nice haircut, another man who is dressed in a shirt that catches her eye. She notices the guy with that great smile. She sees a man holding the door for a woman, and another who stands up when his date comes back to the table. Women see attitude, manners, if a man is comfortable in his own skin. We can measure what we like about each of these men in a split second. That guy in the blue suit is attractive—I wonder if he's single? Would the man with the beard be polite and treat me like a lady? Does the guy with the black shirt know how to dance? Only then does a woman ask herself if she might want to sleep with him.

A man walks into that same room, looks around, and imagines every single woman absolutely naked! I'm not kidding you. Men think in much more sexual terms. Now unconsciously they might like this one better than that one, this type over that one, blondes more than redheads. Whatever. But their first instinct is, do I want to sleep with her? Will the sex be good? Then they start to notice the clothes or the style.

Men are immediate. They see someone and they want her. Period. They're not wondering if she knows how to cook, or if she will like his mother, or if they have lots in common. Who cares? Men know right away in their heads, and in their bodies. Women are slower in that regard.

That's a good thing to remember, because women drive themselves crazy thinking that their clothes have to be perfect, that not one hair can be out of place, that the makeup has to be just so. They won't leave the house unless they get it all right. Remember that he's imagining you naked anyway.

Simply Be Yourself

You know how some nights you cannot be bothered to do anything but go out and pick up some food to bring home?

You are in your most comfortable clothes, your hair is pulled back, you are thinking about no one. You are the opposite of what chic is. Tonight is not the night when you think you need to be perfect. It's not even in your head to look around and see if there is someone to meet. No, you'll pick up the food, and when you get home, you will put on pajamas and eat it in front of the TV. That's what you are thinking. And then, boom, a man starts to talk to you in line for the food, and you wind up going out to dinner with him.

I hear this story many, many times in my life. Why is this? It's because a man looks at you when you are like that, and he sees that you are being just yourself. No pretense, nothing to get in the way of you. And he is attracted to that. To the real you. That's what men look for, a woman being herself. Yes, he may like the clothes and the makeup and the perfume, but he is much more interested, much more turned on, by what is underneath all that. I'm telling you, the more you can be yourself, the more men will be interested.

You Are Perfect Just the Way You Are

Men tell me that the saddest thing is when women are uncomfortable with their bodies. Men don't notice all the little imperfections. No, not at all. Maybe some silly men are very critical, but most men love their women with the wrinkles and stretch marks and all the other things that women think are so horrible. I have hardly ever heard a man talk about these things. But women don't stop talking and thinking about them.

Men want to reassure their women, but the women won't even hear it. Men say they feel terrible that women put themselves under so much pressure. The men know they aren't perfect and they don't expect their women to be, either. Men see their own flabby skin, and they go about their day. Women see theirs, and they don't know what to do, they can't think, they can't work. They spend hours feeling horrible about their bodies. They put themselves through torture. They think they are crap. Men hardly notice. Men don't sit around thinking that their friends are more handsome or sexier or more attractive than they are.

Women are constantly comparing themselves to other women or to pictures in magazines, and then they think they don't look as good. Even the people whose pictures are in the magazines don't look that good in real life—it's makeup and lighting and having someone fix your hair for three hours, all that kind of thing.

So men wish women would go a little easier on themselves, just be happy being who they are.

The Secret to Making Him Happy

Okay, let's talk about oral sex. Men love it to be done to them. We all know that. I have never heard a man say, "No thank you, honey. I don't like it when you suck my penis or lick my balls." Really, who is that man? But I'm going to tell you what men like even more than that. So many men have told me this and when I ask new men about it, they always agree—they want you to put your little finger in their asshole when they are about to have an orgasm. They want you to press down on the floor of their anus, the area closer to the scrotum.

Now, some women like to do this and there's no problem. You just have to make sure not to put that finger anyplace else until you wash it really well. It can carry a lot of bacteria that could get in your vagina and give you an infection.

But if you don't want to do it, you don't need to feel bad. Here's an easy thing to do instead—rub the area between the scrotum and the anus, but on the outside of his body. It's the same nerve endings, and men love this, too. And women seem more comfortable about this as well. So long as you know it's something your man likes, go ahead and make him happy.

Open Your Mind, Open Your Legs

Now a lot of men tell me that they would like to reciprocate the oral loving, but their women are uncomfortable with this. I know they are right, because some of my clients have said things like, "I worry that my vagina smells," "How do I know if my vagina tastes good?" "I think my vagina is too stretched out from having three babies."

I will teach you a few tricks. First of all, the vagina does not smell bad unless something is wrong, unless there is a lot of bacteria in the vagina that is making a bad smell. If you have that kind of a smell from your vagina, then go to your doctor and find out why. Otherwise, stop worrying. A man once told me, "I have never smelled a vagina that didn't smell delicious." Men are much less concerned with the smell than women are. I'm not even sure what women think their vaginas are supposed to smell like. Flowers? Oranges? No, the vagina has a certain smell, and it's very exotic and erotic. This smell gets stronger during sex, and a lot of men say they love the smell, that it's one of the things that gets them excited. I can guarantee you that most of your vaginas smell absolutely fine. More than fine.

Once you get past that, if you want to know what your vagina tastes like, why not just put a clean finger up in there

keeping clean

When I ask men what is their biggest turnoff, the thing they wish would change in women, guys from all over the world—Italians, French, Brazilians, Greeks—they tell me that they are concerned that American women aren't cleaning themselves well enough down there.

We have to take another few minutes when we are in the shower to clean the vagina and the anus. You take some soap and you get that area soapy, and then you rinse off. You don't use soap inside your vagina, only water. Maybe a washcloth to help around back. It takes no time. But just the way you wouldn't forget to wash your legs, you shouldn't forget to wash your genitals.

and then take it out and lick it? If we want someone else to taste, then why not us, too? It's like serving soup that you haven't tasted yet. You want to know, so do it. It's tasty, right? Okay, so we know that the vagina isn't something strange and scary. If you take good care of it, it looks good, it smells good, it tastes good.

So why not have your man practice oral love on you? A lot of women say the orgasm from oral love is the most intense they have ever had, because it's so concentrated on the clitoris. Go ahead, be adventurous. When your man is doing that to you, let him know what feels good. Make up a signal—like you squeeze

better than kegels

Now I'm going to tell you how to revirginize yourself so you never worry that your vagina isn't tight enough!

It sounds like it would be hard to do, but it's very simple. When you're taking a shower, you put one leg up on the side of the bathtub. Put your middle finger inside your vagina, push up and run the finger around, like you were cleaning your nose. Take the finger out, rinse it off, and then do it again. And again. By that time, the vagina will be getting tighter. After a few times, it's hard to get even your finger in. I tell my clients to do this before they make love. When the man tries to put his penis in, it will be too tight. So you will have more time together, to kiss, to talk, maybe to make oral love. Then your natural wetness will come down and the penis will find its way up into you. The sex will be better than you ever had before.

his shoulder when it feels like you might be coming to orgasm. He'll remember, believe me.

Take a Deep Breath and Enjoy Yourself

None of this can happen, though, if the woman is not relaxed. And that is the number one thing I hear from men—they wish their women could relax more. During sex, they see that the woman is self-conscious about her body or worried about how she is doing the sex, how she is performing. Of course if a man says, "Honey, relax," then your whole body is going to tense up. We are like that. So we have to learn to talk to our men, tell them what makes us happy, whether we need to kiss more or turn the lights lower or light candles. But we also must learn to be sure of ourselves, so that we can turn the lights on and still have fun.

nine

Just Say Yes, Yes, Yes

How to Bring the Fire Back into Your Sex Life

The thing I hear the most from my clients is that they feel their love lives are getting less interesting. Maybe they have been with the same man for a while, maybe they are married for a long time, maybe they have children. Many things can get in the way of a good sex life. They tell me that their relationships started off all guns-on-fire, but as the time went on, it became less and less sexual. I have an interesting way of bringing that fire back into a relationship, but always, when I tell my clients how to do this, they say, "Oh no, I don't think I can do that." And I tell them, stop saying no and start saying yes.

Changing Your Attitude

One night a good client of mine called me at home. "My best friend is having trouble. Please, can you fit her in tomorrow?" she asked.

"Of course," I told her.

The woman came in early the next day. We went into my room and as I was waxing her, we started to talk.

The story she told me is one I hear often: She and her husband had been married for ten years. They had three kids. She used to work but quit her job to stay home with the children. All day she carted the kids around, took care of all the little things in their lives, shopped, got one dinner on the table for the kids, and then later on another one for her husband when he came home from the office. You know, the kind of thing most women do every single day. She loved her family, but she had somehow lost herself.

She talked about how things in their life used to be so easy, but that she and her husband had started to take each other for granted and hardly ever spoke about anything but the kids. She said they didn't really fight, but there was this anger that was bubbling just below the surface. They would put each other down in front of other people, and she had started to turn down dinner invitations because she was embarrassed about how they treated each other. And now they were going on a tropical vacation, and she was dreading it.

She said they rarely had sex, and when they did she was just not that into it. She couldn't remember the last time she'd had an orgasm. And it had been ages since she had initiated sex at all. She said she never thought about it anymore. When I asked her if her husband wanted sex with her, she didn't hesitate. "Yes, he always does. Sometimes I say no, and other times I just lie there until it's over."

Whenever I hear that I want to cry. How terrible to want to just have sex be over. No, a woman has to find a way to enjoy it as much as a man.

I told her that one of the real differences between men and women is that men can have sex anytime, anywhere . . . and, basically, with anyone. They can't fake it, because they need the erection. For most men, it doesn't take much more than just thinking about sex and they get hard very easily.

For women it's totally different. They need to be wooed, enticed. They need to shut everything out so they can concentrate on relaxing! Otherwise they just go through the motions.

Men get into bed and think, *Hmm, there's a woman next to me.* And that's usually all they need! Women get into bed and they are thinking, *Are the kids sleeping? Is the kitchen clean? What do I have to do first thing in the morning?* And those thoughts are not very sexy, not at all.

Women get scared because as they settle into life with a man, their libidos aren't as strong as they once were. And they think that once it goes away it will never come back.

But when you love your man, you cannot let all those things come in the way of sex. This isn't fair to either of you. You need to bring passion back into your relationship, no matter how long you've been together. This is so important, and you cannot let anything get in the way or the relationship will feel empty and sad.

Think of Yourself as a Woman First

This new client was shaking her head. She didn't know what to do. But I told her to throw out those bad thoughts from her head, those thoughts that her marriage was over, and to plan as if this trip was going to be wonderful. I told her to pack all her bright, colorful, sexy dresses and some little skirts. Forget that she was the "wife" and just think of herself as a woman. And as a woman, wouldn't she want to go to a fabulous sun-soaked island in the middle of the winter?

I told her to get some lingerie. Nothing slutty, but some nice teddies and well-fitting sexy underwear. It's so funny how wearing something little is so sexy and leads to good things. So buy some new lingerie and wear it. She didn't need to think of herself as a prostitute, but rather as a sexy woman who happened to be with a man she wanted to have sex with, a man she loved.

At night, when they were in bed going to sleep, I told her

that she should let her leg wrap over his, but very carelessly, as if it was completely unintentional. Just the act of being close to him might change her attitude.

Do Not Shut Up!

I told her that she should spend a lot of time talking with her man. Talk is very important in a relationship, and it is one of the first things to go in most marriages. When people live together, they stop talking a lot because they think they know what the other person is going to say. One says something, the other grunts, it goes on like that. Very bad for a relationship. But there are ways to bring back the fun of talking.

The first thing is to start listening. That's right, that's the most important part of talking. If everyone is waiting for the other person to finish speaking so that they can say something, no one has fun, no one learns anything new. So listen, and remember not to nag, and think of new things to talk about. A book you read last week, or a movie you want to see, something light. Nothing serious. No talking about the kids, no talking about the day-to-day problems you might have. Think of funny things, happy things, things that will make you laugh. And just talk, talk, talk.

I told her, if you don't understand his work, then ask him about it, find out what he does all day. If he likes baseball, learn a little about it. You ask questions, you ask what happens with that ball, with all that running around, you make yourself a little knowledgeable. This isn't such a big thing, so don't act like you are the martyr. Big deal, you learn a little about what he likes. You would want him to do the same for you. No matter what the subject—work, sports, family—be genuinely interested and listen with your ears and your mind and heart.

Tell him some funny stories that you never told him before. Sometimes after you've been with someone for a long time, they think you can't surprise them anymore, that they know everything there is to know about you. When they find out that's not true, it makes them realize that there might be a lot more they don't know and they get interested again.

Don't be clingy with him or ask if he loves you. There's nothing worse than that. Because as soon as you ask that question, you give away all your power to the other person. And whatever he answers won't be the right thing. So assume he loves you and go forward.

Now's the Time to Take a Deep Breath

I told her, if your husband isn't having any fun at home, he'll go someplace else to have it. This isn't a secret. Everyone knows that if they're miserable, they won't go back for more. Even a dog knows this. I don't mean that your husband will necessarily have an affair, although that's possible. What I mean is that everyone needs to feel good, and if you're always nagging, always angry, always telling him what he did wrong, then why would he want to be with that? He might as well spend more time at work. Or with his friends, or at a bar. Anywhere but with you. So you have to make sure that when he's with you, he's enjoying himself. And that you are, too.

I told her to remember the things that used to make her and her husband laugh, and to do those things. Sometimes it's just a silly joke or a song that brings back only good memories. Sometimes it's just planning a meal together, or remembering to ask what he might like instead of assuming you know.

I said she should relax. Forget about the kids, forget about whether this relationship is going to work out, forget about all the things that worried you most days. And just be with him.

learn to be spontaneous

There has to be spontaneity in any relationship, but sometimes that's hard when you've been with the same person for a long time. But the more you change things up, the better you feel. It doesn't have to be big things either—just the talking and listening can seem like it's brand new if you haven't done it in a long time. Or maybe you turn on some music at night that you both used to like, but haven't heard in a long time. Maybe you take his hand and you dance.

The most important thing is to make it seem new and exciting.

Make him feel special, make him remember you love him, that you find him sexy and interesting. The funny thing about this is as soon as you treat your man as if he's sexy, he returns the favor.

Go Slow

So okay, there she is, in this beautiful place, with the man she loves. What to do now? I told her to let sex happen slowly. Don't rush it or act like she's had sex with that same man hundreds and hundreds of times.

And then I told her one of my favorite sex secrets. Whenever I tell this to my clients, they are always shocked. But then they do it and they always come back to tell me how much they love it. I tell them to buy some Vick's Vapor Rub, and right before they start to have intercourse, to rub a tiny little dab of the Vick's on the clitoris. Yes, this is really what I tell them! It feels a little funny at first, warm and tingly. It makes the clitoris a little numb, too. But when your man slides his penis into you, it brings a little of the Vick's up into your vagina, and it feels unbelievably good for you. For him, too, because it warms his penis as well. And if he doesn't know it is coming, he will be so surprised and happy. It's just one of those things, like an ice cube in your mouth when you have oral sex with him, that feels so good, which you and he will remember long after.

I thought about that client the whole time she was gone. What would happen? Would it work out for her and her husband? Would they be able to rekindle the feelings? I was so concerned. About a week later I saw that she had booked an appointment for a full waxing. I couldn't wait to see her. As soon as she walked in, I knew the answer to my question. She had such a smile on her face. "So?" I asked. "We had a ball," she said. She told me what a great time they had and how she felt her relationship was right back on track. She said that the sex was amazing, and that they never left the room! Somehow I knew that this was the beginning of something great for them, that sometimes when we think things are the worst they can be, we find out that something wonderful is waiting for us to discover. And that's the best part of life.

Should I Stay or Should I Go?

I have many clients who tell me, "My husband doesn't satisfy me in bed anymore. Do you think I should have an affair?"

Now this is a loaded question. Do they really want me to tell them that yes, they should have an affair so they can be satisfied, too? No, of course not. What they are really asking is how to get what they want.

There are many ways to get to the same place. And when it comes to sex, I see that most women don't speak up, don't lead, don't say what they want. They become less interested in having sex because they are busy taking care of the kids or working or tending to everyone else's problems. A lot of times, their men think they are happy even when they aren't. Is this his fault? No. He just needs to be schooled, and it's up to you to be his teacher. The thing to do is to subtly say what you want.

One way to do this is to just move your body to where it will feel best. If your husband wants you to perform oral sex on him, and you like doing it, then turn around so your vagina is near his mouth. Men often tell me that they would love to perform oral sex on their girlfriends, but a lot of time the girlfriend says no. Or they try and the girlfriend squirms out of the way, telling him that she doesn't want him to do this. Men don't understand why, because I have yet to meet a man that doesn't like oral sex to be performed on them. But what man wants to be turned down? So they stop trying. When I quiz my clients about why they don't let their men do this oral loving to them, they say they are worried that they might not smell that good or taste that good. I have to tell them that unless something is wrong with them, their vaginas will taste and smell just fine. And oral sex feels so wonderful, so why wouldn't you want to have him do it? And if you've got a Brazilian wax, oh my God, it feels great. Better than great.

Sex brings us together. It makes us happy. Why not enjoy as much sex as you can? Believe me, it's never going to make you feel worse.

Pretend

So, how can women enjoy sex as much as men do?

I tell them it all comes down to one word—"pretend." When I say this, woman always get very angry. They tell me that they can't do this, that it feels dishonest, that they won't enjoy it. And I laugh. Because I know that they will enjoy it. Oh yes.

I tell them to imagine that they are many, many people inside that one body. It's easy to do. Sometimes Janea is tired and wants to curl up on the sofa in her pajamas. She's had a long day. But if my man wants to fool around, I remember a girl from my town named Anita, who loves to kiss. And I let "Anita" be a little more adventurous than Janea might normally be, a little more forward. And then there I am, enjoying myself.

The fantasy of sex is fantastic. Any time, all the time. But if you are too serious, the sex doesn't come out as well. So if it's fantasy we want, let's make it the best fantasy. Today, I'm not Janea; today I'm going to be Claire. Claire likes her body, she likes showing it off. She is the sexiest woman in the world, and she wants her man to tell her so. I can bring Claire to the bedroom, and boom, boom, boom, the sex is fantastic.

No More No

There's an expression in Brazil, "You don't know you're hungry till you start to eat." You might say, "No thank you," but then someone brings out this gorgeous plate of food, and within a minute you're picking at the salad and then maybe some potatoes go on your plate. Nibble, nibble. And then, a little while later, the meat. Soon you forget that you weren't hungry, and all you can think about is how delicious that food is. Give me some more please.

Well, sex is the same. If you keep saying no, if you keep thinking you don't want it, and if you keep pushing your man away, he will stop asking. He will forget about pleasing you, and you will forget what it's like to be pleased. And women tell me that when that happens, they feel like they have lost something very important. They feel rejected and then they start to pull back even more. They always assume that once that spark is gone, they can never get it back. But that's not true.

I had a client who was at a crossroad in her relationship. She loved her husband, but she didn't want to have sex with him. She told me that they used to have sex all the time, but as their lives went on, every single thing got in the way—she had to be at work early, or the kids needed her help with their homework, or she was just not in the mood. She was worried that they might be headed for a divorce, but she couldn't figure out what to do.

I told her that she was going to have to change only one thing—no more saying no. From now on, say yes. Every time her husband made the slightest motion toward having sex, she should do it.

"But, but, but . . ." She was thinking of all the reasons not to do this.

I said, "Listen, if you are in love with your man, you have to fire up your sex life again. No doubt about it. Now, maybe some men don't want sex, and neither do their wives, so everyone is happy and they go on with their life without ever thinking of sex. That's a simple thing for them. But you and your husband are not those people. If only one of you wants sex and the other doesn't, you both have a problem. It's not just his problem. And if you don't start to enjoy having sex with him, you both lose. He will look for affection in other places, or you will both become bitter and angry."

And then I told her to have sex with her husband every night for one month. Every single night, or maybe in the morning.

You should have seen the look she gave me.

"I can't do that. He'll know something is up."

Oh yes, he'll know exactly what is up!

If you want to have good sex, then for one month you should have sex every single night. Yes, that's right. One night it might mean bang, bang, bang—intercourse very quick. The next it might be mutual masturbation. Maybe the next day you give him a blowjob. And then maybe the next he gives you a massage. One night you maybe just kiss for fifteen minutes.

Remember: Sex is not like running a marathon. He doesn't have to cross the finish line every night. There are lots of things you and your husband can do to feel good, but his having an orgasm doesn't have to be the ultimate goal. If he doesn't have one, fine, there is always tomorrow night. If he knows he's having sex a lot, he won't be worried about that anymore. He will start to think of sex in many other ways.

The more you initiate sex, the easier it becomes. Maybe you're not in the mood one night. Do it anyway. Don't begrudge him his desire. Feel good about it—he wants you. He wants to have sex with you, he wants to feel closer to you. These are all good things. So no complaining, no acting like a martyr, no rolling your eyes because you are doing something you don't want to.

The more times you have sex, the more relaxed you will become. It's that simple. Once that pattern has been established, you both will start to look forward to it and enjoy yourself. Some nights the sex might last for half an hour, some nights only five minutes. That doesn't matter. None of that is important. Just like women know that size doesn't matter, they also know that quality is better than quantity. Nobody should be watching the clock.

The more sex you have, the more easily you will have orgasms. Why is that? Because you cannot have an orgasm when you are tense and worried. Maybe men can but not women. No, we need both our minds and our bodies to be relaxed in order to feel good. And the more sex you have, the less tense you will be.

I didn't see my client for about six weeks. I was thinking about her every single day, trying to imagine what was going on in her house. I hoped that she was having a good time, and that she was starting to think of sex as one of the real pleasures of life, something that she and her husband could share and look forward to.

At her next appointment, she was carrying a big bouquet of flowers. When she handed them to me, she said, "From my husband." Whenever I see her now, she gives me a big hello from him. She looks better than she has in years.

ten

My Man

And Why I'm Still Single

Every day my clients say to me, "Tell me about your man. Your man must be so much fun, your man must be so nice, your man must treat you so well . . ."

My clients assume that if I have all this experience to give, it's because I have a very good relationship. They figure that I must have taught my man how to please me, how to keep me happy. And that we must have a wonderful relationship.

And it's true—my man is all those things and more. My man is funny and smart. My man loves his job. My man is good in bed. My man is wonderful to me.

The only thing is, I didn't find my man yet!

Too Young to Know What I Had

I was married when I was only twenty-two years old. And even though I was so young, I thought I knew everything, that no one could ever teach me anything. Whatever you asked me about, I had an answer. My husband also thought he knew everything. So already we were butting heads, because we both had to be right all the time. We never let the other one instruct us or lead us anywhere.

In the beginning we were happy. He was a good husband, and a good man. But not perfect. Not one hundred percent. I mean, who is? But back then I was very impatient. I didn't want to wait for anything to change, I wanted it now, now, now.

We had a baby girl, and she made us very happy. But I was still wanting more from my relationship, something I couldn't name. I looked at my husband and I could see that he was unhappy. He was searching for a way to repair what we had, too.

I started telling my girlfriends all about it, about how my husband wasn't being good to me, about how he wasn't paying attention, how he was distracted. You know how that kind of whispering takes on its own life. Psst, psst, psst, blah, blah, blah. They were more than happy to give me advice. They loved it, in fact. They would say things like, "Okay, if he comes home from work tonight and he doesn't bring you flowers, then no sex with him for one week. No matter what, no sex." And I would wait for him to come home, and of course he walked right into the trap, because he didn't have the flowers in his hand. Boom, no sex for a week, and I wouldn't even tell him why. Instead of our relationship getting better it started getting much worse. I was an idiot to listen to these women because they were not out for my happiness.

Living Separate Lives

My husband started coming home from work, taking a shower, and going straight to sleep. No talk, no intimacy, no loving. I didn't think he was cheating, but I knew he wasn't thinking about me, either. I was miserable.

When I saw that things were really bad between us, I knew I had to do something to get his attention. I still wanted to save this marriage, but I had no idea what might work.

I thought about it for a long time, and then I decided to try to make him jealous. I thought that might bring us closer together. So I acted like I had a crush on this dentist that we knew. He was a man that we knew personally and professionally. He was handsome and my husband fell right for the story. He became very loving toward me. It was the best we had been together in a long time.

A few weeks after I told my husband about my feelings for the dentist, my husband played beach soccer like he did every Saturday. That day my husband doesn't play in the game, he is the referee. And the dentist also came to play. Early in the game my husband called one foul on the dentist, and a little while later he called another. The dentist started to argue because he hasn't done anything wrong, and then my husband red-carded him, meaning that he threw the dentist out of the game. The dentist started to yell because he had no idea why this was happening to him, and just like that, my husband threw him out of the league for six months!

We had a few months of things being good, but then they went back to the way they had been. I had tested him for everything that I wanted, and still we were not happy. It was a great lesson to me, because even though I was young, I realized that you do not risk the thing you hold dear just to prove that you can manipulate someone. I did a bad thing, and it haunted me for a long time.

As much as I said I wanted intimacy with him, I held back the most important parts of myself. I never told him what I was really thinking, I never let him get close to me, and I never got close to him. I wanted him to read my mind. I wanted him to be even smarter about me than I was about myself.

I had no patience for trying to change things, no patience for when things weren't perfect. I tell my clients to be a woman, not just a wife, because that's where I went wrong. I forgot that I should listen to him, that I had to be there for him in the same ways I wanted him to be there for me, maybe dress up some nights so we could have fun together, maybe ask more about what his day was like. I was his wife, but I forgot to also be a woman.

Looking for the Right Man

I did date after I got divorced. I think maybe I dated the whole horoscope of men. I had short-time boyfriends, and others that should have been longer but weren't. But the happier I was with myself, the more I enjoyed my business, the more I put myself first, the more I realized I didn't want a man so badly.

And I wasn't willing to compromise. You meet a guy who is good in bed, and once he knows that, he doesn't want to go to work, he doesn't want to do anything else. Or you meet one who is very rich, and he thinks that's enough for you, he doesn't have to do anything else, just have money. He doesn't learn how to listen or to take care of his woman. Or one is lovely but he doesn't like sex. All of them seemed like they were just one part of what I was looking for, not all of it. So the more comfortable I got in my skin, the less I looked for a man.

You see, I'm picky. I don't want to settle. I want a man to make my life better, not worse. So he'd have to be special. But I'm special, too, so why not?

Why I Want It All

There is this four-sided Brazilian symbol that I always think about. On the top it says Work. On one side it says Respect. On the other side, Understanding. And on the bottom is Love. The symbol is to show what we need, that whole package. A little bit of everything.

About the work—I don't care if my man is the president of a big company or the man who cleans that guy's office at the end of the day. I don't care if he makes more money than me, or if I have to pay for most of the things because I make more than him. That doesn't matter at all. What I do care about is that he likes his work, that he does it well, and that he has pride in it. I want him to do that job as well as anyone possibly could. Better than anyone. I don't care if other men think his job is good, or if they think it stinks. I only care what he thinks, how he treats himself. I want to understand what it is he does. Because my work is so important to me, and believe me, he's going to hear about waxing until he could do it himself! So I want to be with the same kind of person.

Then we come to respect. I want a man who respects me as a person and as a woman. He has to know that my daughter and my granddaughter are very important to me, and he has to treat them the way he would want his daughter to be treated. He would have to respect my relationship with them. He'd have to embrace my sisters, too, because we are together all the time and I'd want him to want to be part of that life that we have made for ourselves. We spend every weekend at one of our houses, cooking and eating and talking until the sun comes up. I'd want him to be by my side, enjoying that, too. And of course he would need to respect his own family as well.

As for understanding, now we're getting to the things that

aren't always easy. I'd want him to be able to talk to me about what is really going on in his head, and to listen to me, too. But in order to do that, you have to clean out your mind and not judge every single thing he says. You have to be strong and so does he. You have to work toward the same things, the same goals for yourselves. When times are hard, you have to pull together, not apart. You cannot blame each other and hold grudges. You have to be willing to let go of things that annoy you, and the more important things, too. You cannot be throwing things back and forth at each other's faces, because then you both lose.

And then you come to the last thing on the symbol—Love. This is the hardest part. You have to fall in love with every part of him. Like if he's a very spontaneous man, and you like that about him, you can't turn around later and say he doesn't always show up on time or that he forgot about an appointment because something else happened and he did that instead. You can't fall in love with the part of him that's generous, and then complain when he buys a gift for someone. It's a very hard balance.

I would want to know that I was number one in my man's life. I'd want him to be so proud to walk with me, so proud of what I've accomplished in my life. I worked very hard to get what I have, and I would want him to feel thrilled about what I did—not to envy me or fear that I have more than him. I'd want him to show me off.

Why We Have to Keep Working on a Relationship

I hear women in the salon talking about how they are going to leave their husbands, and when I ask why, they tell me these little things that drive them nuts about the man. I listen, and then I tell them, no, make your relationship better. This is the father of your children. You know him. Why let it go? See if you can change things. Try to do this or that, something you never tried before. Work on it.

Because I know that what doomed my own marriage is that we did not work on making it good. I was too busy playing, too busy trying to make him this way or that. I was more interested in impressing my friends than I was about making it a good, happy marriage. And I hate to see other women make that same mistake.

Some of the women tell me they don't want to "work" on their marriages. I tell them, you have to work to keep the floor clean in your kitchen. Why wouldn't you have to work on your relationship? Is it the most important thing in your life? Yes? Then get out there and work at it. Keep trying new things until it gets better. Fight for it and it will be all the more precious.

Only if you don't love him anymore should you even consider divorce. It should be the last resort, not the first.

Learning to Be Happy Alone

I learned a lot in my marriage. I learned that the wrong man isn't better than no man at all. I learned that I should speak up to get what I want and not to wait for someone to do those things for me. I learned that I am strong, and that no matter what happens I am going to be okay.

I learned that I'm a very good mother and that my love for my daughter made her a strong woman, too. I learned that maybe some people have love and others don't. And that is all right.

I have almost everything I ever wanted. If love is going to come, I will welcome it. But I will not spend any time crying on someone's shoulder about what I don't have. I know now that sometimes it is better to be alone than to be lonely in a relationship.

And the thing I know the most is that whatever comes my way, whatever life has in store for me, I will be able to look it in the eye and make it into something good. That's the Brazilian way.

Acknowledgments

We want to thank our agent, Lynn Johnston, who had the presence of mind to know that we would fall in love with each other and write this book; thanks to Hellene Rodgville, transcriber extraordinaire, who understood every single word; Annie Flanders, for knowing what would work; and Meg Leder and the Perigee/Penguin team, for their support and cheerleading.

About the Authors

Janea Padilha of the J Sisters Salon knew how to shape an eyebrow before she was out of kindergarten. Inspired on a Brazilian beach, she invented her signature waxing technique, and the salon she started with her sisters is now a multimillion-dollar business. Vist Janea's website at www .jsisters.com.

Entertainment writer **Martha Frankel** zipped Jennifer Lopez into her wedding dress, tried on lingerie with Elle Macpherson, and assured Sarah Jessica Parker that some day she really would find a signature role. Her hilarious and heart-wrenching memoir, *Hats and Eyeglasses*, was lauded as "intimate and exuberant" by *O, The Oprah Magazine.* Visit her website at www.marthafrankel.com.